EMBRACE
YOUR PAST
WIN YOUR FUTURE

M000081773

PHILLIP,

PEACE & HAPPINESS

EMBRACE YOUR PAST

WIN YOUR FUTURE

*The difference between
being a victim and playing one*

MARK CRANDALL

Copyright © 2019 Mark Crandall

All rights reserved. No portion of this book may be reproduced in any form without permission from the publisher, except as permitted by U.S. copyright law. For permissions contact: support@markcrandall.net

Cover Photo Credit:
Limelight San Antonio
www.limelightsanantonio.com

Back Cover Photo Credit:
April Piotrowski of Black Mill Photography

Cover Design:
Predrag Markovic

Formatting:
Sandeep Likhar
LikharPublishing.in

Editing:
Spencer Hamilton of Nerdy Wordsmith
www.nerdywordsmith.com

ISBN: 978-0-578-48570-6

More of Mark's Work

Free Course offered:
www.markcrandall.net/whyexercise

Purpose Chasers Podcast:
www.markcrandall.net/purpose-chasers-podcast

Purpose Chasers 7-Day Jump Start:
www.markcrandall.net/Jumpstart

Purpose Chasers Academy:
www.markcrandall.net/PCA

Table of Contents

Foreword

Mark is like the brother I never had. We understand each other and the adversities the other has overcome. Although we faced very different challenges, that passion for transformation beats equally in both our hearts.

Our stories both began in tragedy and are now lived in triumph. Adversity and hardship are things which often shape our lives and how we live. They come in many forms, from harmful, physical, and emotional abuse, to post-traumatic stress and seemingly unbearable childhood trauma. Whatever we may think, harmful environments mold the way we view the world and others around us and they often hold us back.

The greatest limitations are placed upon us by our own minds. Self-doubt, negativity, a lack of confidence, and self-limiting beliefs are all things which keep us locked into the harm which we know does us no good, but which is almost impossible to break free from.

I met Mark Crandall through Rock Thomas's March to a Million mastermind program. However, it was when we met in person at the Unleash the Power Within event hosted by Tony Robbins that I found he was my "brother from another mother."

Mark is a licensed therapist whose story did not start in success, but in severe abuse and the foster system leading to drug addiction, robbery, jail, and, ultimately, prison.

What I love most about Mark's book, Embrace Your Past, Win Your Future, is that readers will find ways in which to change how they view their past and how they create their future. Mark chose his own path to success without knowing the outcome. The key is to challenge your perspective from seeing what happened to you, to seeing it as something that is happening for you to start living your life on purpose. Mark provides a step-by-step guide to turning self-hatred, routed in past trauma and transgression, into a powerful resource for success.

I have personally witnessed epic transformation from the power of this process in Mark's life and that of some of his students.

Are you ready to live your best life on purpose?

#EmbraceYourPastWinYourFuture.

Carolyn Colleen
Author of *F.I.E.R.C.E.:*
Transform Your Life in the Face of Adversity, 5 Minutes at a Time!

Introduction

I am but a man
*   Withered with decay*
I am but a man
*   Who survived another day*

I spent the first twenty years of my life pushing the memories shared in the first eight chapters of this book as far as possible from my conscious mind. The memories I'm sharing with you are those of a child who learned to manipulate belief systems as a means of protecting himself. These belief systems will appear throughout the first section of this book.

Please understand while reading about the situations from my past: my state of mind and thought processes at that time are not consistent with my current perceptions. These accounts do not necessarily depict actual reality, but rather my perception of reality at the time it occurred. I want to bring you with me to the point where I began to embrace a different belief system, one that has helped me heal and live again—for I was not living then, merely attempting to survive.

Sometimes, I am truly shocked that I survived my first two decades. With drug-addicted biological parents battling their own demons, I came close to death many times. Abandonment produced an overwhelming fear of future abandonment, which turned into anger and rage. This manifested itself as destruction—inflicted on myself and others.

My story is one of abuse, neglect, drug addiction, criminal activities, depression, violence, self-destruction, and, finally, a profound spiritual transformation. Statistically, a man walking through life with the cards I was dealt and some of the hands I have played should not be here to write this book. If ever you were looking for a belief in spiritual accounts—God, Higher Power, the Universe, Laws of Karma, whatever you want to call it—may the stories of my life prove to be the truth you have been searching for.

I have found internal freedom from a fiery hell I lived in for many years; it is my hope that all who suffer may seek and find the same.

The second half of this book is a step-by-step guide of how I overcame my past traumas, turned hatred into love and a victim mentality into the fuel to create the life of my dreams. It is my hope that anyone with a dark past may find these words and gain the hope and clarity that they may or may not have even known existed.

Author's Note

I want to start by sharing a disclaimer and an invitation. The disclaimer is that the first half of this book is my story. Although it has been truly powerful for the readers of its first release in 2017, I invite you to skip the new edition, now Part I, if you so choose, and jump to the second half. The second half of this book is how I shifted my mindset from "everything in life happened *to* me" to "everything in life happened *for* me." In this section, I will walk you through a number of exercises and experiences that will allow anyone that reads and applies the teachings into their own lives to break free from their past and begin to build an epic life!

PART I:

Eulogy of Childhood Memories

The reality presented in Part I of this book is the author's and may not align with the reality of those represented. All names have been changed to protect the privacy of the people involved in this story.

CHAPTER 1

Why'd You Leave Me?

Fixated by fairy tales
Separating them all
Built with strong nails
Only to watch the structure fall

My earliest memories, some of the darkest and most difficult of my childhood, are not those I would wish on any child, especially one so young. I was around two and a half years old when I remember a night where I was placed in the living room of some random house to watch television. I remember that I was not interested in the entertainment on the screen at all. This was a common scenario for me.

I have several memories of being in unfamiliar locations with a feeling of being alone. As strange as it may seem, I remember finding comfort in the feelings that were produced from being alone. This is a strong thread that continues throughout the entirety of my life.

This is just one of many memories.

I remember another time. I was sitting watching TV. I heard a commotion in the back room. I remember not wanting to look back, as I felt I would get into trouble if I saw what was taking place. For several moments, I fought the urge to become aware. When I couldn't resist any longer, I looked. At the time, I was ignorant of what it was I saw.

Several years later, I knew that what I had witnessed was my mother and some random folks snorting a powdery substance off a chest freezer. Once I saw my mother and was assured that she hadn't left me again, I went back to watching the show. Even as a child, I was never satisfied with what was present in my life. I was always searching for just a little something else; something to take the pain away, to dull the thoughts, to place me somewhere other than the here and now.

At about the same time, I remember waking up in an apartment in Claremont, New Hampshire, which happens to be where I was born on November 3, 1983. I remember seeing my sister sitting on the floor playing with her dollhouse. There was a knot in my stomach, a strong feeling that something was wrong.

Well, something *was* wrong. That something was that I could not recall the last time I had eaten. I was so hungry. I asked my sister where Mommy was.

"They are at the diner across the street eating," she said.

I punched her dollhouse and started crying hysterically. Mommy had left again, I thought, and she was not coming back.

This world was already so unfair for someone so young.

Shortly after this, my sister had been placed in a bathtub for a bath and nearly drowned as a result of my mother leaving her alone. My grandmother found her and called 911. Learning of that moment many years later, it seemed like a great basis for hatred, and it became just that. The Department of Children, Youth and Families (DCYF) was contacted, and my sister was taken from my mother.

Shortly after my sister was taken away, I have a memory of sitting at a random kitchen table eating some delicious fruity cereal. A strange woman notified my mother of a phone call she had just received. My mother's reaction was one of anger and fear. She ran out of the house screaming and crying. This must have been a common occurrence, as I remember not even slowing down the process of shoveling cereal into my mouth. Actually, the cereal appeared to taste better.

I believe the phone call that instilled panic in my mother was from DCYF, as they were looking to take me from her as well. Of course, at the time I hadn't the slightest idea what this meant, nor could I anticipate the amazing blessings that would unfold as a result. A few weeks later, I was placed in the same foster home that my sister had been placed in.

Many years later, I was able to confirm that the call my mother received was DCYF notifying her that she needed to bring me in because they had a home for me. The strange house that I was in at the time was somewhere in New York. My mother had fled New Hampshire in an attempt to keep me in her custody. DCYF had called the foster parents who took my sister and asked if they would consider taking me as well. They agreed. My foster mother said that I showed up to her house wearing pajamas I had outgrown and carrying a small trash bag full of belongings, none of which fit or were useful to a child who was going to stay away from home.

For several years, I heard nothing of my mother. I spent so much time trying to answer the riddle of "Why?"

Why hadn't I heard from her? Is this love?

Imagine pondering thoughts like these at the age of four.

I later learned that she sent us cards and drew us pictures. My foster parents were concerned about the impact it would have on my sister and me, so they withheld them. I know now that they did this because of the inconsistency of my mother's contact and the empty promises that she spilled on each page she sent. It did appear that our mother seemed to have more interest in us while we were gone than she ever did when we were in her custody.

Reflecting back, I did not know or understand what was going on during this time. The only thing that kept playing in my head was that Mommy had left again. It has taken years of spiritual practices, therapy, and a number of various transformation courses that have allowed me to now have some freedom and compassion for what she was going through. But before that, I took it all out on her.

Where the fuck was my father? Why didn't he take any of the hatred shots I so often fired at her?

On later reflection, I feel it was at this point that I unknowingly made a vow to never be hurt by another woman. This was an attempt to protect myself from feeling abandoned. It would sabotage every subsequent relationship.

Although I was placed in the care of a loving and embracing family, I couldn't feel the love that they shared. I just knew deep down that they would leave me at some point. Everyone had up until this point, so how could this be any different? I remember staying with my new grandparents while my foster parents worked on leveling land for the new trailer that they purchased. Unaware of it at the time, I was to be raised in this trailer, outside of trips to institutions and other fine establishments intended to rehabilitate unwanted children such as myself.

I also had no idea at the time that these memories, although scattered and vague, were the beginning of an umbrella of self-pity and hatred I would live under for more than twenty years.

In the following chapters, I will discuss various situations I found myself in as a result of playing the victim and blaming every action that I took on events from my past, while fighting an unwavering internal battle.

If only I had the outlook then that I have now, I could have saved so many loving people from the heartache and turmoil that was left in the wake of my destruction, set in motion by my determination to take what I felt the world owed me.

The downside—or upside, depending on your perspective—is that if I had made different choices, I might not have walked as far through hell as I did . . . and surely would not be as strong as the man writing this today.

CHAPTER 2

Something is Wrong
with This One

Lay me down and tuck me in
  Played the game and couldn't win
An expensive lesson I had to learn
  Every bridge crossed I chose to burn

Most people can only imagine what it is like for a seven-year-old to try to explain to his classmates that he doesn't know his real parents, especially when he doesn't fully understand it himself.

I tried to comprehend the role that these "fill-in" parents were playing. I used to tell the other kids in class that my mommy was going to come back and get me soon. These bad people took me away from her. Because of all the medications I was already taking for what the doctors deemed depression and ADHD, even at that age, I would pretend that I was some kind of science experiment, and the findings of the research being conducted were held on another planet.

"Try this counselor with this combination of medications. He surely has ADD and Bi-Polar Disorder. Something is wrong with this one."

Not knowing what any of this meant, I just wanted my mom and dad to come back and get me.

Living with my foster parents was strange. I always had food to eat, which although I couldn't put it together at the time, was new. I used to eat entire boxes of honey buns, and other "fat kid" snacks. It was as if in my mind I needed to eat as much as possible because I was unsure of whether or not the food would run out. My new parents never said anything; they just kept buying more snacks. However, no matter how much I ate, I never got full.

I developed a low self-image. It was difficult for me to pull my shirt off around other kids. I wasn't fat, but I had developed a little gut. This is more than likely due to all the oatmeal cream pies and honey buns I had consumed over the past three years.

I struggled to fit in. I was enrolled in soccer, which I really enjoyed. It wasn't the actual sport that excited me but the hopes of getting to kick another kid in the shin as hard as I could. Watching others suffer brought me a sense of joy, knowing that they would experience even a small piece of what I endured on a daily basis.

Around this time, I met my first friend. James was a super cool kid, which I couldn't understand. He lived in a trailer just like I did. Many kids poked fun at me for living in a trailer, but not him. After one of our meaningless soccer games, he invited me over to his house to play. I remember running around outside with him, playing "war," which looked like us smacking each other with sticks and using cuss words that I couldn't get away with saying at my own house.

I felt connected to James. All my fears and worries about how the world was going to fuck me over each day went away. Unfortunately, I could not be such a comfort to James. He made the mistake of showing me his Ninja Turtles collection—the most lavish Ninja Turtles collection I had ever seen! He had them all, even the limited-edition ones that I was begging my foster parents to buy me. Nothing they ever bought for me was good enough. No matter how hard they tried, they could never show me enough of the love and affection I craved. James had one Ninja Turtle that I wanted so badly. I tried to convince him to let me borrow it, but I think he knew how shady I was even at such a young age. He would have never seen that Turtle again.

One day when I was picked up from James's house, I remember begging to go to the store to purchase that Turtle. I was told no and that if I wanted to own that Turtle, I needed to save my money to buy it. I never enjoyed being told no (even to this day, it's one of my least favorite answers). On Monday, I went to school like normal. I remember bringing one of my Turtles for show-and-tell. James brought his as well. The little shithead just *happened* to bring the Turtle I wanted to borrow for show-and-tell. I looked so stupid. James made a fool of me, and that I couldn't let stand. At recess when all my classmates ran to the door to go play on the playground, I headed for the bathroom. My teacher pleaded with me to go outside with the rest of the kids. I said I just needed to go potty, and then I'd go outside.

I didn't need to go to the bathroom; James needed to suffer. My mission was to take his prized Turtle from him. I felt excitement. Adrenaline shot through my body as I walked to my coat on the rack to hide the Turtle. When recess was over and everyone came back in the classroom, I tried to act normal. I was attempting to disguise my devious actions. A few moments passed, and everyone became fixated on the fact that James was crying. He found out that his favorite Turtle had vanished. This was my friend. He was one of the only kids who had invited me into their home.

I'm sure most children would have felt a strong sense of guilt or shame, or, at the very least, a recognition that stealing is wrong. Me? I felt complete. Any concern about my friend was quickly replaced by an inner joy.

As an adult, I now understand that a child deals with the belief that "everyone will leave me" by preempting that move. By *purposely* causing someone to leave, you're not the victim. This episode was one of the first in a pattern of pushing people out of my life in an attempt to protect myself from the impending turmoil that I would suffer when they inevitably left.

As my childhood progressed, it continually brought me a real sense of satisfaction to watch others suffer. As an adult, I know that often people steal because they need to. I stole because I enjoyed watching people suffer; I enjoyed watching them go through all the stages of loss.

"Where did it go?" I asked.

"I must have lost it," James replied.

"It was just here."

"Did you take it?"

"Who, me?"

"Yeah."

"No way! I would never do such a thing. Let me help you look for it."

This one experience led to a life of stealing. Sometimes it was an object such as money or clothing, and later turned to stealing drugs and anything that would allow me to purchase more drugs. My most common theft was emotional security, which was usually stolen from those who cared about me the most.

The first memorable feeling of inadequacy struck me hard in the first grade. I remember sitting at the little tables joking with some kids in class. We'd always read out of a book right before naptime. I really enjoyed naptime. Jocelyn and I would lie beside each other and pretend we shared the love of two movie stars. Well, at least that's what *I* pretended; who knows what was going on in her little mind. Somehow, I always seemed to avoid the book making its way to me. This day was different. My class clowning was interrupted by the teacher handing me a Dr. Seuss book. She asked if I would start the reading.

I started to try to read the words on the page but couldn't. I stared at the letters on the pages but couldn't make them into words. Classmates started to laugh as I struggled through the pronunciation of each letter that made up each word. I couldn't do it. I was unable to read. The laughter tore through me like a freight train. The shame and horror I felt was instantly replaced by rage and hatred. I took the book from the table and threw it across the room and launched a chair at the chalkboard. My classmates and teacher were alarmed.

This situation set the tone for how I would respond to life for many years. When confronted with any challenge, my auto-reply was to insert rage. This was demonstrated through a number of uncivil behaviors, which I quickly found out society frowned upon.

I was sent to the principal's office for this outburst. Mr. Pebble was a feared man. Very soft-spoken, with bright red hair. I wasn't even nervous. I actually felt as if I were cared for, as if I were noticed. The reason why I was in his office didn't matter to me. The end result of the conversation was that I now had to attend sessions with a reading tutor. This tutoring was so conveniently taking place during the time of reading in class; this meant that I did not need to worry about the book being passed to me again.

Later that day, all the kids were out on the playground. We were all running around, and one of the kids, Spence, made a comment about how I was unable to read the book in class. I don't remember his exact words, but I do remember the rage that shot through me as the other kids laughed. I picked up a large stick and threw it as hard as I could at Spence. Due to the fact that I wasn't an athlete of any kind, the stick fell short of Spence and struck an innocent girl. It split her head wide open. She started screaming; again, everyone appeared horrified at my outburst. I remember countless people asking what was wrong with me.

I was back in Mr. Pebble's office and was notified that my foster father was on his way to pick me up. I was being suspended from school for a week—not the norm for your average eight-year-old. Well, as I'm sure you have determined on your own, I was clearly not your average child. The suspension actually brought me some comfort. My foster father showed up, and all he said to me was "Get to the car." His punishment for me was to sit in the recliner for the next five hours until my foster mother got home. I don't remember how the situation ended up playing out, but this started the torture that I was to put my foster parents through for the next seventeen years.

For the next couple of months, I had to go down into the basement of my school to take a reading practice class. I hated this time each day. The woman that I had to meet with had the smelliest breath ever, and she would sit so close to me that I wanted to vomit. Although extremely uncomfortable, I became motivated to learn how to read, if only to not have to meet with Dragon Breath any longer. (That's not her biological name, just an assigned pet name.)

Focusing on people's faults and shortcomings is a tool I embraced early on. I formulated negative opinions about everyone that I came into contact with. These formulations would comfort me as I moved through life, the comfort being that if they were to leave me, I had already built up a story to justify the abandonment.

Dragon Breath ended up making a recommendation that I be transferred to Canaan Elementary due to their special-needs programming. My foster parents complied and agreed with this request, and I became a SPED. This is what all the kids were called that needed either academic or behavioral assistance in school.

Just one more reason to feel inadequate.

CHAPTER 3

New, More Responsible Humans

You picked me out of a line
  Not knowing what was in store
You chose me and accepted me
  Like an eagle, one day I would soar

October 31, 1990, was a day that I will remember as long as I live. Outside of the fact that it is my biological mother's birthday and three days before my own, it was the day that my foster parents decided to adopt my sister and me.

Of course, at seven years old, I had no idea what this meant. I just knew there was a celebration, and everyone kept congratulating me. I was so confused. I'm being congratulated because my biological parents could not take care of me, and now some new, more responsible humans were picking up where they left off? This baffled me! Imagine being seven years old and attempting to explain to your classmates what had just transpired, especially when it made no sense to you. I'm unclear on what I said, but I know that my own confusion must have only muddled it for others.

Although the adoption process was one of the most confusing things I went through as a child, it later proved to be the most amazing blessing I could have imagined. Two incredible humans agreed to accept my sister and me into their home and completely uproot their lives to raise us. Sounds easy enough, but knowing what I put each of them through, it is a blessing that I have the relationships that I do with each of them today. My new mother taught me about unconditional love and the power of prayer and positive thinking. My new father taught me how to work hard and provide for your family.

Shortly after the adoption, I was transferred to Canaan Elementary School to take part in the Special Education Program. I found myself feeling like even more of an outcast. As a result of the compounding confusion, my behavior spiraled even further out of control. I was on a quest to drive everyone as far away from me as possible and was about to face a whole new group of people to whom I would have to explain what was going on with me and my life, when I couldn't even put it together for myself.

As part of being enrolled in the Special Education Program—or SPED as the "normal" kids called it—I was able to access the SPED room at any time throughout the day. This was convenient because my behavior was escalating. I would skip classes and roam the halls. I created a number of disturbances, including but not limited to disrupting other classes by being a clown, throwing things, damaging property, assaulting other kids, stealing, and on and on. I learned that if I dropped the SPED card, it would prevent me from receiving consequences for my behavior. I used this to my advantage every opportunity that I had, whether it was getting out of homework assignments, going out for an extra recess when all the other kids were in class, or avoiding suspensions. It did not take me long to realize that this setback was an extremely beneficial tool.

As I began the new school, I thought I was starting to be accepted by the other children. Instead, it turned out that they were terrified of my extremely unpredictable violent tendencies. I didn't think twice of kicking a kid on the playground, throwing a chair, slide-tackling someone in the hallway (a skill learned from my mother's attempt at getting me to play soccer), and so on. My group of friends shifted completely. I started to build meaningful relationships with all of the other SPEDs, most all of whom were engaged in the same "fuck the world" attitude that was taking root in me.

CHAPTER 4

Anything that Takes Me Outside of Myself

It's not your fault, I swear
      You weren't taught to care
Opened scars laid bare
      Much too painful to share

Around this time, I began to explore my sexuality. Although sexual exploration by children and young adolescents is rarely talked about, I feel that my memoir would lack the integrity of my life if I didn't share some of my experiences.

My adoptive parents brought several other children into their home during my childhood. I can think of at least ten who came to live with us. My room was always the one that was shared with these guests. The "roommate" that most sticks out in my mind was my cousin Michael. He was eight or nine years older than I was. At the time, I was around nine, and Michael was seventeen or eighteen years old. His companionship was the start of my sexual exploration. He demonstrated many things that a nine-year-old probably shouldn't see. We shared bunk beds (and of course, I was on the top, since his age trumped mine). I remember countless nights when I would wake up to my bed rocking and sounds of some heinous animal attack down below. I had no clue what this was until my curiosity became overwhelming, and I began to go through Doug's belongings in our shared room.

I found a pile of magazines with nearly naked women on the covers. I remember flipping through the pages and something started to happen in my pants. I don't need to go into detail, as I am positive that we all know what goes into the creation of an erection. I had no clue what was going on with my pants situation until I started to explore and quickly realized that if you rubbed it hard and long enough it would go off. The explosion was the most profound experience of my life up to that point. Since my parents worked long days and opposite shifts, I lacked supervision. As with many boys that age, I started to rub my little willy on anything and everything.

This led to further surveillance of my cousin and his lower-bunk sexcapades, the discovery of more pornographic material, and telltale stains on nearly everything I owned and some of what others owned. Needless to say, I was far advanced in my knowledge of sex compared to my peers.

In school, I always had a girlfriend and would try to re-enact the things that Michael did to his girlfriends. When you are ten and eleven years old, this is severely frowned upon when you are caught. For more background on this, feel free to ask my foster mother. Poor woman. At age twelve, I was dry-humping everything in sight. I got caught dry-humping a couple of relatives, "playing house," and even a six-year-old girl I was forced to babysit a few times.

Of course, I know today that this behavior is not okay and I am remorseful for many of my actions as an adolescent. I don't remember ever being educated on what was acceptable sexually and what was not.

I remember my adoptive father telling me to "wear a condom, or you may get something that won't wash off in the shower." I had no idea what that meant at the time, nor did I care. I knew that when I climaxed, it made me feel good. As with most of my behavior in my early years, I never stopped to consider the ramifications of my actions on others; I was solely concerned with finding relief.

To this day I am still remorseful for many of my attempts at seeking relief, but I do know the importance of educating my children on what is acceptable and what is not. For example, it is not appropriate to go down a girl's pants in first grade. I learned that the hard way with a suspension from school.

Having counseled and coached hundreds of men throughout the years, I now know how common such behaviors are, and also how detrimental they can be to the transformation process of forgiveness. This is the sole reason why I have placed this section in my story.

CHAPTER 5

Santa's Not Coming

Forever seems so far away
When I can't even end today
Hearing voices, seeing no faces
Demons inside my hunger chases
Open your eyes, there's no time to dream
Not everything is the way it may seem

I remember the Christmas Eve of the year my sister and I were adopted more than any other. We were told that our biological mother was coming to visit us. We hadn't seen or heard from her in years. I remember the excitement. My sister and I were running around the trailer, jumping up and down with sheer joy. Every time there were headlights on the road by our house, I would run to the sliding glass door to look outside. Each time there was a growing feeling of disappointment, as it was only a car driving by. I can remember my adopted parents making several attempts to draw our attention away from our growing disappointment.

Looking back, my adoptive parents may have been hurt by our excitement, but they also anticipated our inevitable disappointment and hated that we had to experience it. Our biological mother did not come that year. She continued to lay the groundwork for me to be convinced that no one could be trusted. Especially women. They lied.

Looking back on it now, and knowing all about the addiction, I know she probably *wanted* to show up. If she was suffering from addiction, as I would later, no matter how badly she wanted to show up, she couldn't.

Our biological mom did come the following Christmas. We visited her in her apartment with her boyfriend of the week. I remember our ride to her apartment in Claremont. Again, my sister and I were so excited. I remember thinking how impressed she would be to see the boy that I had become. Once she saw me and got to know me, she would change her mind and want to take me back.

You must remember, for a child, the most precious relationship is that of your parent. Very little, including the worst neglect and abuse, can totally dissolve the desire for a parent's approval. While we were taken away from her for good reason, it would be years before I stopped looking for her approval.

I don't remember a lot from the visit, but what I do remember ended our ability to see our mother for many years to come.

My excitement to be around my mother was on some next-level shit. I was absolutely out of control at her apartment. I don't remember what my sister was up to, but I know I couldn't shut up about the candy Mom had bought us. I was begging and pleading with her to give us our candy. My mom was starting to get angry, and even more frustrated was her boyfriend. As a result, they believed that it would be a great idea to put me in timeout. This was done by handcuffing my arms behind my back—with real handcuffs—and placing me in the closet outside of the kitchen. I remember being in that dark closet, crying, terrified for my life. I mean, for fuck's sake, I was a child. At that moment, I remember regretting my inquiry into wanting to get to know my mother. I wanted to go back with my adoptive parents. I don't have a solid recollection of how the remainder of the visit went, but I know that we were rescued by my adoptive parents.

My adoptive mother later explained that when they arrived at the house, they pounded on the door for almost an hour, waiting for my mother and her shithead boyfriend to give us back. My adoptive mother confessed that she felt uneasy when dropping us off, and that she and my adoptive father drove around with an uneasy feeling the entire duration of our visit.

I was told that after about an hour, my mother answered the door and let me out of the closet. My adoptive mother states that I ran out of the house, screaming and crying, and hid behind them while the boyfriend grabbed my sister from inside and threw her down the stairs. My sister has cerebral palsy and had just had surgery on her legs and were in casts. Needless to say, we didn't see my biological mother again for at least five or six years.

My rage and hatred toward the world intensified greatly. I started punching holes in the wall at home, swearing, and stealing daily. I rarely followed the rules and guidelines set by my adoptive parents. I did not care anymore, and I'm sure that was evident by my behavior.

CHAPTER 6

Traits of a Serial Killer

Why do I feel so incomplete?
Am I destined to fall to this defeat?
Spirits of darkness arise from within
Why is it so comfortable every time I sin?

After the visit with our biological mother, it was decided that it would be best to enroll my sister and I back into counseling. As usual, this also included some new diagnoses and a host of medications.

As a child, I often refused my medications. They always made me feel strange and different—*different*, of course, being the root of *strange*. This meant that I would be seeing a new counselor. This was a common occurrence, as I seemed to go through counselors like toilet paper. My new counselor was a man named Fred. I had had many counselors through the years, but Fred was different. Our relationship lasted for several years. I would go each week and drink hot cocoa and play chess. I didn't beat him until our final session; I'm still convinced that he allowed me to win.

At the heart of these visits were conversations surrounding my behavior. My parents used to go in and visit with Fred before I did. They would tell him all the terrible endeavors I had engaged in that week. Looking back, it was necessary because around the ages of nine and twelve, I really started to spiral out. I was assaulting people, throwing furniture, killing frogs from the pond by my house, and setting fires. Setting fires excited me beyond belief. The experience of spreading gas or some other accelerant around, knowing that as soon as you put a flame to it there would be the wonder of how much damage it would do . . .

Read that last line again. This is a metaphor; although it makes sense here in this chapter, it will make more sense later in this story.

In 1992, my adoptive mother became pregnant. Due to infatuation with myself and my quest to find some relief from my internal suffering, I was oblivious to what this would do to the attention that I was constantly seeking from my adoptive parents. A few months into her pregnancy, my adoptive mother caught my adoptive father cheating on her; second time, same woman. I remember a pretty heated argument resulting in him leaving. During the argument, my adoptive father said he would not come back as long as I was still living there.

This crippled me. I folded up on the inside. Everyone who stated they love me leaves. What the hell is wrong with me? Am I such a bad person?

He did end up coming back right before my new little brother was born in February of '93. I clearly remember the day my brother was born. More important than that, I remember the excitement of finding out that my adoptive father was moving back in.

Shortly after my celebration of having my family back, my adoptive parents split up again. My adoptive mother was now working full time and trying to raise a new baby. I remember her being super upset one evening, and my adoptive father was not there. I asked what was wrong, and she angrily stated that my adoptive father had continued to cheat on her. I asked what was going to happen to me.

My adoptive mother stated, "No matter what happens, I am always going to be here for you. I'm not going anywhere, and neither are you."

I really wanted to believe her, but based off past experiences I was unable to do so. This conversation was the start of a downward slide of which I am grateful for every day I came out alive. With my adoptive father gone, I lacked supervision after school until my adoptive mother got out of work at night. This meant as soon as I got off the bus after school, I would get into as much mischief as humanly possible.

The year was 1996, and I was thirteen years old. I went outside to play. My "play" at the time is not something you would see on television or view out your kitchen window. I was on a mission to cause destruction, with the intention to subside some of my internal suffering. I headed down to the shed that was behind our house. It provided enough cover to hide my mischief from unwanted attention.

An idea had struck me on my way down that I should fill my winter plastic sled with accelerant and set it on fire. I did just that. I laid down a trail of accelerant heading to the sled. When I lit it, there was a massive explosion. It set several items surrounding the shed on fire, including the side of the shed itself. There was this overwhelming sense of fear that the shed was going to burn down, or I would set the forest on fire.

I loved this feeling and welcomed it.

I was able to throw buckets of water on the shed to put that out and attempted to hide the rest of the damage. When I felt complete, I ran inside to pretend as if nothing had happened. I was scared of what had just happened but became accustomed to these feelings and enjoyed the thrill of whether or not I would get away with it.

Later that evening, the police came to the house. My grandmother had been mowing our backyard and discovered what I had done. The police officer stated that I was in trouble. This was not a new interaction for me, as my adoptive father had caught me stealing several times and for some reason always found it necessary to bring me to the cops. The officer stated that he would be calling my adoptive mother to discuss how to handle the situation.

When my adoptive mother came home from work, she seemed mortified with what I had done. Here I was thinking it was magical. She stated she was calling my counselor Fred to set up an emergency meeting. I was unsure of whether or not I was supposed to be nervous, but I wasn't. I was excited to see my counselor again; after all, he was the only one that seemed to understand what was going on with me.

Later that week, we went in for an emergency appointment with Fred. Although divorced, my adoptive parents were both still heavily involved with my therapy. They went in before me, which was normal, but this time they stayed in there an unusually long amount of time. Finally, the door opened, and Fred came out to the lobby and asked me to come into his office. He didn't seem to possess the same excitement to see me that he normally did. My parents were still in the room, and I asked why that was the case. I was a cocky little shit with a "get away from me" attitude written all over my face everywhere I went. Fred stated that my actions had forced my adoptive parents to make a very difficult decision. He stated that he had recommended months ago that they file a CHINS petition on me.

"What the hell is a CHINS petition?" I asked.

Fred stated that I would be going to a group home, where I could receive the help I needed.

"Yeah right, I'm not going anywhere."

He explained that I had a court date in two weeks, and at that time I would more than likely be leaving from court. After our meeting, I didn't give the court date much thought at all. I continued acting and doing how and what I wanted.

The court date rolled around, which happened to so conveniently take place on the last day of seventh grade. My adoptive father stated the night before this date that he would be waking up at 9:00 a.m. to bring me to court. I disregarded his demand and got on the bus and headed to school.

Around 9:00 a.m., I was called down to the principal's office. Having been suspended from school several times, I was no stranger to the principal's office. Apparently, it was not okay to throw a stapler off the forth-story balcony, or pour a bottle of Tabasco sauce into your teacher's coffee, or shoot tacks at your classmates. These kinds of behaviors were not tolerated and led to numerous suspensions from school.

As I was walking down to the office, I couldn't think of why I was making this trip. Usually when I was called down to the office I had such a long list of things that it could be for, I wasn't able to pinpoint just one. Today was different. I hadn't done anything at all (that I could recollect). Of course, it was the last day of school, so it could have been for anything.

When I approached the office, my adoptive father was standing there. He looked at me. "Let's go, you are late for your court hearing."

"I am not going," I said.

He grabbed me by the arm and nearly dragged me out to his car.

I was shipped to Jefferson, NH, which is in the middle of nowhere. I remember arriving there and not really understanding what was happening to me. This was not uncommon, as I felt this way every day.

CHAPTER 7

Packed Bags

Frustrating himself
*   With thoughts of pure evil*
Overpowering all that's right
*   Absolute hatred and hostility*
So unbearable

In the year that I was a ward of the state, my internal dialogue really started to fire on all cylinders. I began to reflect on the meaning of life, to really contemplate my existence. The lie that started to expand in my thoughts was that of how everyone who had ever stated they loved me had abandoned me. They left, walked away, stated they were disappointed in me. I questioned whether my life held any meaning at all. Many nights I would lie awake in bed and ponder thoughts regarding whether anyone would miss me if I weren't here. Would anyone even acknowledge my disappearance? It was starting to sound like an easy solution to the daily internal dialogue within my mind. Although today I know that I was suffering from clinical depression, back then it felt like a constant state of darkness that followed me everywhere I went.

My roommate in the second group home was a kid named Ben. He was cool, constantly getting away with mischievous behaviors that I always seemed to get disciplined for. Ben started to educate me about sex, drugs, and rock and roll. We often stayed up late listening to inappropriate music Ben had snuck in from visits home and discussing the fuckery that the world had cast upon us. When he was talking, I was his student. He talked about how much pot he smoked before being trapped in this place, and how he was smoking on his visits and passing his drug tests when he came back to our little home away from home.

I knew of pot due to my biological father smoking it on the couple of visits that I had had with him. In that setting, it was not attractive to me at all. My biological father's life was nothing that I ever wanted. I had subconsciously decided in my youth to avoid any actions that could possibly lead to me living the existence of my biological father. Even the few times that my adoptive parents let me visit with him as a child, I never felt connected to him. It was almost as if I'd withdrawn to the idea of knowing him. I never understood my resistance toward him, especially contrasted to my insistent yearning to know and have my mother in my life.

When Ben talked about smoking pot, it appeared to be what I had been missing all along. The pure joy and excitement that would take over his entire being when he discussed it allowed me to possess a sense of relief. I could not wait to try this magical medicine. I used to hound Ben to bring a sample for me from one of his visits back home. Every visit he stated he would, but every return was a letdown.

Behind the house where we were being held against our will, Ben and I would go sledding and hide in the woods, smoking cigarettes and launching snowballs at passing cars. He snuck an album back in from a visit that absolutely changed my life. The album was *40oz. to Freedom* by a band named Sublime. The first time he played it, I felt as if I were being carried away. Bradley, the lead singer and author of all the magical words that filled the poetry in every song, got me. It was as if he understood what had been going on in my head. What I didn't know was that one of my favorite songs off this album was written regarding Bradley's struggles with heroin addiction. This would become clearer to me later on in my life.

One of the strongest memories I had about this placement—outside of the fact that my adoptive mother hated the place—was the fact that every single Friday my adoptive father would pick me up and drive me back home. Every Friday he would pick me up and buy me a soda and chips. It was the greatest feeling of all time—finally waiting for a parent who actually showed up when they said they would.

Ben ended up going back home before I did, but my memory of his influence on me lasted for many years. A couple of weeks after Ben left, I had a court date. Court dates had become so common for me that I didn't think anything of it. It usually meant that the judge would lecture me on my behavior and send me back to the facility I was at or plan my trip to the next facility. This day was different. My adoptive mother made an argument in court for my return home. She stated that I had already missed half a year of high school and should integrate back into society. The judge agreed and released me back home that day. My overwhelming excitement wasn't for going home, necessarily; the excitement was for the opportunity to experience all the glory that Ben had spent countless hours prophesizing about.

I remember having a couple of weeks before school started back up. I found a job washing dishes at a local truck stop, as my adoptive mother required that I get a job since she was gone all day at work. A couple of weeks before school started, I hounded my adoptive mother to take me to the Polo outlet, so I could wear the clothes that all the "cool" kids were wearing in my group homes. She obliged my request and spent hundreds of dollars on clothing for my new start. I really wanted to do well in school this time. I liked school. I mainly enjoyed literature and philosophy. I thoroughly enjoyed reading and writing.

It was unclear to me at the time, but both of these tasks took me out of the torture chamber within my mind. I thought that by dressing nicer and gelling my hair, it would completely transform the lost little boy within. What I didn't know at the time was that this attempt was similar to the metaphor of polishing a turd. Yes, you can polish a turd and make it shine real nice, but it still smells like shit.

My first day back at school was not what I had made it out to be in my mind. Before homeroom had completed, I learned that my classmates had voted on a nickname for me before I went away. That nickname was "the psycho." Although it was entirely accurate based off of the behaviors that I often displayed, it crumbled my very existence.

By lunch I had started to identify the kids that may have access to and potentially sell me a bag of weed. James (my old BFF—you know, the one I stole the Ninja Turtle from) and I started talking during science class. He asked me all about my "vacation," and I anxiously told him about all that I had learned. James stated that he had a bag of weed and asked if I wanted to go to his house to try it out after school. I remember thinking that I would rather skip school and try this now! The rest of the day couldn't pass quick enough. I left several classes to find James in the school. I was like a creepy stalker. I looked through countless windows each period until I had him in my sights. He wasn't going to leave me. Not on my watch. I needed to experience the glory that Ben had described for hours every night.

School ended, and I ran out of the school to meet James in the parking lot to walk up to his house. He invited a few other kids that I knew from before leaving. All these kids used to be out of my reach as far as friendship was concerned. They were popular, and I was anything but. Up until then, no one wanted to hang out with me because my behavior was too unpredictable. I was a loose cannon.

James and the other three kids and myself walked up to his house as if we were on a mission from God. Nothing, and I mean nothing, was going to stop me from experiencing the glory of smoking this magical plant.

When we arrived at James's house, everyone walked out back to his father's tool shed. They seemed to know what they were doing, so I followed their lead. James pulled out a bag of green stuff that smelled like a skunk's ass and put a chunk of it into a metal thing. It looked like the pipe that the caterpillar from *Alice in Wonderland* smoked out of. James put the device to his lips and set the green stuff on fire. He sucked it into his lungs. Within a couple seconds of his pull, he was coughing and spitting all over himself. Everyone including myself started laughing hysterically. It appeared that he was going to die. His eyes glossed over and he had snot bubbles coming out of his nose. I remember thinking in that moment that despite all the hype Ben gave this stuff, it didn't appear to be all that magical.

James passed the pipe to me, and I pretended I knew what to do. Well, it was almost as if I did. I put it to my lips, applied fire, and took a pull off it as if my life depended on it. Little did I know in that moment that my very existence for the next ten-plus years was going to depend on it. As the warm smoke filled my lungs, I began to gasp for air and started coughing uncontrollably. James stated that the only way to get rid of the cough was to take another pull as quick as possible, and so I did. I pulled even harder this time, and coughed harder. My eyes grew warm and my nose started running with the same snot bubbles I witnessed from James.

Then ... all of a sudden, I began to experience the most overwhelmingly powerful body and mind sensation of my life up until that point.

There was a sense of peace, a calmness that took control of me. My mind stopped. A heavy haze settled my thoughts, and in that moment, I couldn't even recall anything. It was glorious. Just as Ben had stated it would be.

The rest of the evening was hazy, to say the least. I remember going in James's house and eating snacks until we felt sick to our stomachs. For the first time in my life, I felt like everything was going to be okay. Everything was exactly how it was supposed to be. The thing that I didn't take into account was that it wasn't going to stay that way.

The effects of the pot wore off a couple hours after returning home. I immediately phoned James and asked if he could get me a bag of weed. He stated he could, and I could grab it from him tomorrow at school. I was so excited—my very own bag of weed! Ben would be so proud of me.

From that day forward, my high school career consisted of having and/or being around those who had weed. My friends became all the kids that I vowed to never hang around due to their resemblance to my biological father. None of that mattered. The cost of association was outweighed by the amazing and enchanting effect produced. I began smoking weed every day, all day. I started skipping school if I didn't have it so that I could find it. My grades slipped, but that was not a concern to me. The only things that mattered at that point were having a job so that I could buy more weed and smoking to release my mind.

CHAPTER 8

Defining Obsession

Touching the blade
> *Feeling the thrust*
Penetrating the skin
> *Breaking all trust*

I had been in many relationships with women in high school, but nothing meaningful. There was a steady yearning within each one to run before it was too late.

At the time, I was unclear and unaware of why this was so, but, to be honest, it didn't matter. All I cared about was staying stoned every waking moment of my existence.

After work one night, I was hanging out with some kids from the grocery store where I worked. We were driving around in my car, smoking weed and listening to music. One of the kids received a phone call from some girls who wanted us to go over to their house and smoke with them. We headed over. I remember that Lane, the kid who received the call, had a crush on one of them. When we pulled up to the house and the girls ran out to my car, I remember being engulfed with fear. This one girl stood out from the other two. Her name was Karen, and she was amazingly beautiful and made me stumble over my words. I was in love. I had an immediate need to have her in my life. Unknown to me at the time was the fact that this was Lane's crush. I'm not sure it would have mattered if I did know.

We smoked, laughed, and talked. I fell deeper in love with Karen. She was so intelligent and beautiful. Although she was kind of sloppy from drinking wine she had stolen from her father, she made my heart skip beats. It's as if time stopped when I was in her presence. We left after a few hours. I ended up getting her phone number before we left that night. Lane wouldn't shut up about all things he was plotting to do to Karen sexually. He went on and on. Clearly, he was unaware of the fact that I had fallen in love with Karen and was going to make her mine.

I called Karen the following day to see if she wanted to go out on a date. She stated that she did. She asked me if I had any weed. I made her aware of the fact that I sold weed, and therefore never did not have weed. I wasn't selling it to make money—I rarely did, except when I ripped off some younger kids.

I picked her up, and we went down to my favorite spot by my house. It was a private beach on Mascoma Lake. It still holds a special place in my heart due to all the family functions that had been held there over the years. Our date consisted of smoking a ton of weed and fooling around in my backseat. We stayed there for hours. I drove Karen back to her house and upon leaving, I felt this weird sensation come over me. A sensation that I did not experience again until meeting my wife over ten years later.

I talked to my adoptive father about my experience the following morning. My relationship with my adoptive father became much stronger after the divorce. I turned to him with all my questions, as most children do with their parents. (Well, everything outside of the amount of pot we smoked.) That morning, he gave me a very crucial piece of advice: "Mark, wrap your meat, or you may get something you can't wash off in the shower." He then proceeded to the bedroom and found a box of condoms for me. He asked if I knew how to use them, and I told him I did. I had no idea how to use them, or exactly what the riddle he just shot at me meant. It didn't matter, because shortly after that conversation, Karen called me and stated that she couldn't see me anymore.

I had an instant pit in my stomach that stayed with me that entire day. My world just fell in around me. I didn't know how to respond at first. Then, out of nowhere came this overwhelming hatred toward her and all women. My adoptive father used to tell me that all women were lying whores. I didn't want to believe him, but it was appearing to be accurate. All the hatred I held onto toward my biological mother came back. I remember screaming and swearing at the sky, hoping that Karen would experience the worst that life had in store for her.

Karen called me the following day to tell me that she had changed her mind and wanted to hang out with me again. In a single instant, all the self-judgment I had been wallowing in, and the hatred of women vanished. I asked her if she wanted to stay over at my adoptive father's with me. I told her I pitched a tent in his yard, and we could stay out back. My adoptive father argued with me regarding the plan that I had established, but I knew he would give in, and my adoptive mother would stand firm in her conviction that I was too young to have women spend the night. Karen stated that she was excited, and we set a time for me to pick her up.

I will spare you the graphic details of the events that unfolded, but will state that I lost my virginity. Karen and I were inseparable from that point forward. "Inseparable" is kind of an understatement. Karen turned into an obsession. I craved more and more of her in an attempt to quench the thirst within. Although I was always left dehydrated.

Each day I was consumed with thoughts of what she was doing, where she would be going, who she would be hanging out with. I didn't know it at the time, but I was viewing my relationship with Karen through the lenses of the relationship I had with my biological mother. I had a deep-rooted fear that Karen would just vanish one day. Without a note or an explanation.

School was no longer a necessity, nor was work. I began skipping both of these and would stay at my friend Austin's house all day, smoking copious amounts of weed and drinking liquor from his parents' cabinet. Austin and I began hanging out all day, every day. We had so much in common. Catching a buzz consumed my life; but not just catching a buzz—reaching oblivion.

There was something about Austin that really intrigued me. It could have been his knowledge of various narcotics and the results that they would produce on the mind and body, or the fact that he had also been to group homes and had a similar childhood. Our common bond was a shared hatred for the world. Austin taught me about snorting pills, taking ecstasy, drinking liquor, assaulting people, robbing stores, and many other important life-adaption tools that would come in handy.

It was around this time that my consumption of narcotics outweighed the amount of money I was bringing in each week from my part-time position at the grocery store. Because it was cutting into my weekend partying schedule, I ended up quitting my job. They were fed up with me, anyway. I was notorious for sucking the aerosol from an entire case of whipped cream cans, going out to push carts and disappearing for an hour or two, and not making my shifts on time or at all. My life consisted of finding and consuming as many substances as I possibly could.

One day, completely out of money and without a job, I made the decision to sneak into my adoptive mother's bedroom while she was in the shower and take a little money from her purse. As I was doing this, my brother snuck up behind me and screamed to my mother in an attempt to notify her of what I was up to. I turned around to tell my brother to shut his mouth, and he screamed again. I punched him in his face and left her bedroom with the money. When my adoptive mother got out of the shower, she was furious. She stated that she knew I had been taking money from her purse but was just waiting to catch me. She started crying, saying that she had given me everything I ever wanted, but it was never enough. She told me she knew that I had a drug problem, and I needed to leave her house.

I didn't think anything of it, as she had made this statement before but lacked the follow-through for it to become a reality for me.

I drove over to Austin's house that morning in my shitty car that only had one gear due to my lack of upkeep. Because I rear-ended a car at a stoplight after nodding off on sleeping pills, the bumper was held on by a bungee cord. The car leaked power-steering fluid, but by now I was used to driving a tank. I remember I used to hammer on it to see if I could blow first gear out of it, even took it on the highway a few times. If you ever heard a vehicle on the highway doing 65 mph in first gear with an exhaust leak, you'll know it is a beautiful sound.

When I arrived at Austin's, I never mentioned the incident with my adoptive mother and brother. We just proceeded to do what we always did. Smoke weed, take a few shots of liquor, eat snacks, and talk shit. His parents always threw me out when they got out of work. Apparently, they were not big fans of coming home to find me always at their house, combined with the fact that they usually couldn't see through the veil of weed smoke. Today was no different. At around 5:30 p.m., his mother returned home from work and told me to "get to steppin'," and so I did.

I headed home, completely forgetting what had happened earlier that morning. I arrived home, and within five minutes heard a pounding on the door. It was the police. I opened the door, and they stated that I needed to leave the house, that my mother had called in that I was trespassing on her property. I swallowed hard. I had nowhere to go, no place to call home. Instead of owning what I had done, I started cursing my adoptive mother for what she had done to me. I quickly got a bag of belongings together and headed to my car. The police kindly made me aware of the fact that my license had been suspended for an unpaid speeding ticket so I was not to drive my vehicle.

I called my friend Todd and asked him to pick me up, explaining to him that my mother had thrown me out, and I had nowhere to go. I wasn't clear with either Todd or his parents about exactly what had gone down at my mother's. I knew that if I told them I was a thief and that my mother had finally caught me, I would not be able to stay with them.

During this time, Karen and I had broken up. Without my car, I wasn't able to drive to go see her, and apparently she didn't think enough of our relationship to put the effort in to come see me. I didn't care anymore.

It was at this time that I started having daily thoughts of ending it all. The hatred toward my biological parents overwhelmed me throughout each day.

"They did this to me."

"This is all because of them."

These were common delusional states that I lived in. I had spent a majority of my life blaming others for every situation I placed myself in. I always found someone else to blame—and if you had the childhood I did, it wasn't hard to find a scapegoat.

Playing the victim was a position I stood in for many years. I could easily get others to feel bad for me and my situation. I had so much practice using lies and manipulation to show others just how the world had wronged me. It was easy . . . until I had burned every bridge leading anywhere in life. I'm not at that point yet in my story, but it escalates quickly over a four-year period.

CHAPTER 9

How Many Bottoms Are There to Hit?

I remember a time when I could stay afloat
Thought I would be doing the world a favor if
I slit my own throat
Perfect planning on my part,
I've just written the introduction to my suicide note
Wait, that's not what I'm trying to say . . .

Todd's parents treated me like their own son. They fed me, clothed me, and made sure I got to school on time. One of the bonuses of living at Todd's was that his older brother sold pot. I was always making myself at home to his stash.

One night we had a party out on Todd's land and invited a ton of people. Per usual at these functions, I ended up getting black-out drunk. I don't remember much of the night, other than the fact that Karen and a couple of her friends, who I referred to as the "hoe train," were there.

I woke up on a strange bathroom floor covered in puke with a massive headache. I managed to lift myself up to look in the mirror. My face was black and blue and covered in blood. Someone heard me rustling around in the bathroom and came to check on me. It was Karen. She looked mortified.

"What the fuck happened?" I asked.

"You got in a fist fight with Todd's brother and wouldn't stop, so he ended up snapping a tree branch across your face."

I felt it. It had to have been a thick one. I reached in my pockets to find a pocket full of weed. I was not sure where it came from, nor did I care. I always woke up with pockets full of other people's stuff. This was a game I played at parties. I liked to see how much I could steal from others.

Karen drove me back to Todd's house. I was surprised to find his mother and father greeting me at the door. They had all my belongings packed and out on the porch. They said that I could no longer stay there and that I had been nothing but a problem since I moved in. Karen, feeling bad for me, invited me to stay at her house.

We started "dating" again. I viewed it as a place to live, which included sex and food. I hadn't drawn a sober breath in well over a year at this point. I was consuming whatever I could get my hands on, whether I bought it or stole it. At this point, with only one week until graduation, I dropped out of school. My teachers stated that I would graduate if I just showed up. Well, I couldn't do that. I just wanted to end it all. I began obsessing about taking my own life. Karen would go to school, and I would wheel and deal all day to make sure we could get high when she got out of school. That was my job, and one I excelled at.

I started stealing from Karen's family—whether it was money off the counter, which was placed there for her brother's lunch, or money out of a stash-spot her father kept in his bedroom. This lasted for quite some time. They never said anything to me, which I enjoyed.

One day I called a kid who I frequently bought weed from. He stated that he didn't have any weed at the moment, but did have something better than weed. He had me at "better than."

The combination of weed and alcohol really took me outside of my mind, and even at barely eighteen years old I was fully addicted. I couldn't stop or moderate even though I had tried on several occasions. I asked him what he had, and he said he would pick me up in an hour. Back at his house, he pulled out a stack of little wax baggies containing some brown powder. I had no idea what it was, but was curious to know what the hype was about. He stated that sniffing one of these baggies was the equivalent of smoking a blunt.

"Well, I might as well smoke two blunts then. What's that going to cost me?"

"Ten dollars per bag," he replied.

"I'll take two then."

I cut open the two bags of powder I had just purchased and poured them on the top of the glass coffee table. I snorted them in one massive line. I remember the feeling as if it were yesterday. Within a couple of minutes my body was tingling. My eyes slanted, my mind stopped racing. It was the most amazingly euphoric feeling I had ever experienced. I asked what I had just done—something a normal person probably would have done in the beginning.

"Heroin," he replied.

Oh my God! I thought to myself. I was never going to do that. Only junkies did that stuff. Losers like my biological parents. Those thoughts lasted only a moment or two, and I settled back into the amazing feeling that was heroin.

The kid drove me back to Karen's house. A couple of minutes into the short ride back, I asked him to pull over, as I was about to get sick. He jerked his car over as if he had done this a thousand times before, and I jumped out, oblivious to all those around me. I sat cross-legged, puking my brains out. It felt so good. When I got done, I felt as if I was even more intoxicated than I was before I got sick. He dropped me off back at Karen's, and I called him every day, multiple times per day, to get more and more of that magical drug. I even cut down on smoking weed.

When Karen's parents had had enough, they called the mom of one of Karen's friends, and I went to stay with them. I stayed with them until I stole a debit card and withdrew a few hundred dollars from their account. They asked me to leave, as everyone else had. I was a loser, and I knew it. I was an addict, but I was less willing to admit that.

I couch-surfed around the area, staying in a half-dozen places, none of which lasted that long. I continued to steal from and fight with people. I was absolutely out of control. I was on a suicide mission. I had thought about dying so many times, but couldn't seem to muster up the courage to do it myself. I figured one of these nights of being under the influence would be my last.

I had acquired a job working for a packing and moving company— if you call it *working*. I was constantly stealing from the place: selling packing boxes to people and not ringing them up, taking money from people and giving them a truck to rent without putting it in the register or ever filling out the proper paperwork. My life was pitiful, although it felt normal. I really imagined everyone on Earth going through the same daily struggles.

I went into work one day, but this day was different. I had nowhere to go after work. I had a phone with all kinds of numbers programmed in, but knew that none of the individuals in there would pick up if they saw my number come up. This is the place in which many reach their bottom. One man's bottom always seemed to be an even greater reason for me to get loaded. I stole the entire deposit from that night's business transactions and walked out with zero intentions of ever going back.

After leaving, I walked around the city hoping to see anyone that might have a substance that would relieve me from the way in which I felt inside. My mind was racing. I became more riddled with fear with every car that passed. Multiple people wanted to hurt me for the actions I had taken against them or someone that they knew.

This is a cleaned-up way of saying I had fucked over every single person in my life and was known all over the area as a scumbag. A reputation rightfully deserved.

I was able to get my hands on a couple of 40oz. bottles of booze and a handful of pills. After the first 40oz. was down the hatch and the Xanax kicked in, the morbid thoughts dissipated. I had forgotten that I had just taken $900 from my job and the rest of the world wanted me dead. I began to think about my next options.

Without much effort, I remembered that I did have one friend left. Austin! I hadn't talked with him in several weeks, but nonetheless I called him. The explanation of how I was down on my luck and walking the streets was a common story, and there wasn't much difficulty on my end getting it out to others. Austin stated that I could come live with him and his girlfriend until I got on my feet again.

I was nineteen years old and had one friend left. Austin was the only person in my life that I hadn't burned—at least that I could remember. Austin came and picked me up. When I got in the car with him, it was as if we had never missed a beat. I gave him a couple of the pills I had acquired and we smoked a couple of joints on the way back to his apartment.

While I lived with him, his girlfriend, and their daughter, I got a job at a pizza place down the road. Once again, the money I was earning was less than the money required for me to stay loaded. His girlfriend worked at the local gas station. Austin and I would go there almost daily to steal alcohol and other items. We had a good little racket going for a bit. It was not long before I was fired from the pizza place for coming in late and under the influence. It was a crappy job that paid minimum wage anyway, I rationalized.

Without any money coming in, my relationship with Austin started to dwindle. We weren't talking much on a day-to-day basis. He and his girlfriend would take off all the time and leave me in the middle of nowhere.

One day I was completely out of money and had nothing to take me out of my head. The stores in the area were catching on to the fact that I never spent any money but went in several times per day; it was too risky to steal anything. I started rummaging through the house. The long and the short of it is I ended up finding $550 in a cereal box. Not knowing what this was or whom it belonged to, I took it. I bought some booze and a pack of smokes. Then I got some pills.

This was the most devastating point in my run with substances. I didn't get any relief. I drank a 12-pack, ate a handful of pills, and smoked two pretty good-sized joints. Still, I could not stop thinking about how I had just stolen from my only friend.

It was a couple of days before anyone noticed that the money was gone. Of course, there was the usual chaos surrounding things that I stole.

"Where did it go?"

"You didn't take it?"

"It was just here, and you were the only one home."

My defense was always the same: "I would never steal from you." That line had been used so many times I couldn't even say it with conviction any longer. Austin had to pawn his PlayStation and some other belongings to come up with the money to replace what I had stolen. Turns out it was his sister-in-law's rent money.

I just wanted to crawl into a hole somewhere and die.

Each day I woke up hoping that it would be my last. Yet each day I would end up catching a buzz that would keep me until the following day. Around this time my cousin Freddy came into the picture. This was my adoptive father's nephew. He had me come stay with him a couple of towns over.

Freddy came to pick me up at Austin's. I had a couple of bags packed and was on the porch ready to go. Austin didn't even say goodbye to me, nor did I make eye contact with him. Austin's girlfriend was working at the store, so I decided to stop in and get one final take. This take was a little advanced from the rest. I decided to take around ten cartons of cigarettes and several cases of beer. So much stuff that I had to make a couple of trips back to Freddy's car. (Oh, and a case of Slim Jims. I always took Slim Jims for some odd reason. This seemed to be my trademark.)

When we arrived at Freddy's house, I quickly learned that he had three other roommates. Although I was thrilled to have a place to stay, Freddy's roommates didn't appear to share my excitement . . . until I offered up my stolen goods—then everyone became much more hospitable.

I slept in the living room for four months, but paid no rent and contributed nothing at all. This was my first bottom. The lowest of lows—so I thought.

During this period, I was drinking cheap vodka daily, bottle after bottle. I ended up getting hired by a painting company. I lasted for about a month. There appeared to be some promise once I got a job. Most days I would arrive at the shop unable to walk in a straight line. This didn't bother them at all; they just were not going to let me drive a company van.

The end came on my last Friday painting. I hadn't eaten in days due to not having any money. I came back to Freddy's house, angry as all hell. I had been drinking all afternoon at work and taken some pills and smoked a truck full of weed. I started drinking vodka like it was the last bit of air on Earth. I have vivid memories of blasting "Sober" by Tool in the basement. It was on repeat, and I couldn't stop crying and kicking and punching holes in the wall. I wanted to die, and if I had had access to a gun in that moment, I more than likely wouldn't be sharing this account today.

When I woke up in the morning, Freddy and his roommates confronted me. They stated that I had a problem, and I had better get help.

I was stunned. Completely puzzled by their statements. I needed help? These dirty hippies were in the same state as I was. This offended me. *I need help . . . not even sure what the hell that means.*

They then told me I was no longer allowed to stay with them. Then it hit me. Here I was again, same place as always.

Ever since birth:

People giving up on me.

People throwing me away.

People tossing me out with the trash.

I couldn't think of anyone to call at this point. It was over. Maybe I should just jump off a cliff. No one would miss me if I did. I had a thought that was not of me. It was as if a guiding force passed me a note that read *Dear shithead, call your grandparents—they will help you.* I wasn't sure it would work, but I was willing to give it a shot.

I picked up the phone and called my Oma and Opa. Opa answered the phone with excitement. It was almost as if they were expecting my call. This was the first time I had asked for help. It wasn't a place to stay, but genuine help.

"Opa, I'm in a bad way. I have nowhere to go and don't even want to live any longer."

"Where are you? I'll come and get you."

CHAPTER 10

Cry for Help

I am but a man
  Withered with decay
I am but a man
  Who survived another day

When I arrived, my Oma had a dismal look on her face. She appeared to be distraught and disappointed. She told me to go get cleaned up for dinner. In that moment, I felt a glimmer of hope. Although it was short lived, it was enough to keep me from taking my life.

I agreed to refrain from using any and all drugs while I lived with them; I eagerly agreed, unaware of the fact that this wasn't a possibility. I was, however, allowed to drink beer.

Two days after living there, Opa wanted to go hiking. I wasn't a big adventure guy, but the plan was to pick up some beers and go hiking. Anything that had to do with beers sounded like a good time to me. I remember drinking way too many beers. My backpack was full when we left and empty before we got to the top. When I got home, Oma just shook her head and said, "Before dinner, Mark? What is wrong with you?" I didn't know the answer to that riddle. I just knew that I felt so hollow inside all the time and the only relief I had ever found was through ingesting alcohol and other substances.

I was also starting to figure out that no matter how many or how much I intended on having, I always overshot that. Usually there had to be some separation from the alcohol or substances for me to stop—generally, intervention by someone or something, as I was unable to stop on my own once I took any mind- or mood-altering substance into my system.

I managed to get two jobs while living at Oma and Opa's house. One of which was sanding drywall for a large construction company. I enjoyed this job because it afforded me an environment to drink and do as many drugs as I wanted, as long as I could get my tasks done. I was provided two raises in pay while there for my hard work. I also took on a job at a local pizza place making pizzas after I got out of my drywall job. My Oma was budgeting my money for me, buying my smokes and giving me spending cash each week. She learned after the first paycheck that I did not possess the skills to do that on my own, and she surely didn't want me living with her forever.

Probably a month into living with my grandparents, I was having some severe tooth pain. This wasn't a surprise, as I hadn't seen a dentist in years. My Oma made me an appointment to see a dentist. They were unable to do anything on me that day, as the infection in my mouth was too bad to work on. They sent me home with antibiotics and pain medicine. I didn't know it at the time, but this visit was going to be the beginning of the darkest life I have known to date. The dentist that wrote my prescription wrote me a prescription for thirty 10mg Vicodin with five refills. The refills were not supposed to be on there, but I wasn't going to say anything. I hadn't done an opiate in months, but when I filled that prescription and threw two into my mouth, that feeling returned.

Everything disappeared.

I felt alive, like I could do anything. However, I wasn't capable of doing anything. As I filled those prescriptions just as quickly as they were available at the pharmacy, my life blurred by, along with all responsibilities or care for life.

I had been sober now for three months. Drinking and eating my Vicodin. Things were going well. I wasn't partying or hanging out with bad influences; in fact, I wasn't hanging out with anyone. My spare time consisted of drinking beers and playing video games in the basement of my grandparents' home.

One Saturday afternoon my cellphone rang. I didn't know the number, but I picked up. It was Austin. He wanted to know if I wanted to go to a birthday party with him. I screamed through the phone with excitement, "YES!" I was dying to get out of the house. He picked me up and immediately asked me if I wanted to smoke. I explained to him that I had made an agreement with my grandparents, and I didn't want to disobey them. We arrived at the party, and the beers were flowing. I was pounding them.

The combination of the pills I had taken that morning and the beer had me in a full wobble by noon. On the ride back to my grandparents', I told Austin to pass the weed. I smoked a couple of bowls, and before the second bowl ended, I made the decision that we needed to buy a bag for me to take home.

My Oma had found me an apartment to go look at. She never said it to me, but I was beginning to feel that I was a burden on her and my Opa. My Opa brought me up to look at the apartment, paid the deposit, and made plans for me to move in. I did not have any say in the matter. My Opa decided this was the place I needed to live, and I was moving in the following week. Not that I cared much either way.

Austin came the following weekend and helped me move into my new apartment. Once we had all the furniture and all the things my grandmother had gathered up for me, we proceeded to get wasted.

I was on my own for the first time ever. Quickly I learned that I had no idea how to live on my own. Nothing mattered as long as I had what I needed to feel okay on the inside.

Unfortunately, my prescriptions ran out. I soon learned where to get more. There was a woman down the street that seemed to always have what I needed. I only knew her by her street name, Grasshopper.

When I first met Grasshopper, she seemed like a sweet woman. She always invited me inside and wanted to know what was going on with me. It was never a chew-and-screw with her. There was always good conversation. A couple of days into my frequent visits, she ran out of pills. I was devastated.

"I have something better if you're interested," she said.

I had heard this same phrase before, but was unclear where. Without a second thought I said, "You have some heroin?" I was so excited. I literally felt as if I were high before I had even made the purchase.

Visiting Grasshopper became a more than daily occurrence. Before I knew it, the money my Oma had saved for me was gone, and I was living paycheck to paycheck. I started stealing from co-workers at work, money out of their lockers or drugs out of their vehicles. It didn't take long for them to identify who the common denominator was. I was quickly outcast at the shop. No one would smoke with me on breaks or talk with me throughout the day. This didn't affect me—as long as I could stay under the influence.

Nothing mattered to me when I had my fix.

One day on lunch break I was getting stoned when, all of a sudden, my back went out. I collapsed to my knees. Confused and scared, I tried to stand up but was unable to do so. What the hell was happening to me?

I'm only twenty-one years old at this point. Terrified, I called my Opa and explained to him what was happening. He told me to leave work and go to the hospital. I listened to him and did just that. I couldn't straighten my back and was in a great deal of pain.

The hospital ran a bunch of scans and tests on me. The doctor asked what I did for work and I explained that I sanded drywall with a portable sander. I explained that a majority of the work I did was overhead, meaning I had to sand the ceiling joints on the houses we assembled in the shop. Because this happened at work, they explained to me that it would be a workers' comp case. I was unsure of what that meant. All I heard from that visit was that I was going to be prescribed Percocet for the pain.

Percocet quickly turned into OxyContin and Fentanyl patches.

I was unable to work during this period. I honestly couldn't tell you how much of it was back pain or just a desire to stay within the story I had created to continue to get my medications. My money dwindled as I waited for the workers' comp checks to come in. My apartment went from a clean place I called home to a disgusting flophouse where all the misfits could party. It was gross! Trash was everywhere; a pile of dishes hadn't been cleaned in months and a smell that gallons of bleach couldn't counter permeated the air.

Because of my overwhelming need to buy drugs and alcohol, I fell behind on rent. Each week when the landlord showed up, I would hide. The sheriff's office served me an eviction notice, and I stayed in that apartment until the last day of the notice. I was forced to sell my medications to survive. My existence was completely hollow. I only went outside at night out of fear that I would be assaulted by one of the countless people I had ripped off.

I hated myself. Hated the very thought of continuing to live this way.

And yet, those thoughts disappeared once I got high.

I moved in with some girls who lived across the street from me. Of course, the agreement we made was that I would pay them once my checks came in, and in the meantime I gave them pills from my prescriptions. Although I won the workers' comp claim, I was trading most of my medications for heroin, and my life was completely unmanageable. I missed my final date, which was created to agree on a settlement for my injury. This was likely a blessing, as the amount being discussed would probably have been enough to kill me.

I did receive two paychecks for lost wages of around $3,000. I remember the Friday that they came in. I quickly ran to the bank to cash them. It happened to be the same day that my prescriptions were refilled. This was glorious, as I had the money to fill them on my own for the first time. Which, in drug-addict terms, meant that I could keep all my medication to abuse at my leisure.

I filled my prescriptions and went to the liquor store to meet one of my heroin dealers. I had done a bunch of Oxys that day and had been drinking since noon. When I arrived at the dealer's house, I traded him some Oxys and cash for a large amount of heroin. I snorted three bags and got ready to leave his house.

As soon as I got outside my breathing became constricted. I had to get down on one knee. I remember saying a prayer: "Please, God, don't take me yet." The meaning of the prayer had nothing to do with any life I felt I had yet to live, but everything to do with the drugs and alcohol I had yet to consume.

What a life I was living.

I made it back to the apartment. I gave the girls I lived with some rent money, and we proceeded to party. I felt on top of the world—although, looking back on it now, my life was a complete shit show. I had become the person I stated I would never be, one of my biological parents. I never wanted to live paycheck to paycheck or live each day for the buzz I would acquire. It didn't take long before my money ran out.

I started robbing everyone I had come into contact with. I was crawling through windows, waiting for people to go to work, kicking doors in, pry-barring businesses. It got dark quickly. I was again constantly looking over my shoulder. I didn't want this life. I had so much potential.

The girls I was living with asked me to leave after becoming a few weeks behind on rent and one of the girls "losing" her portion of the rent money. (It wasn't lost—I had stolen it one day while she was at work.) I ended up finding a homeless shelter to stay for a bit until I figured things out. I stayed there for a few weeks and was forced to see a substance abuse counselor.

I had no idea what he talked to me about, as I was wasted during every visit. I do know that the police were constantly there looking for me. I was always being questioned about crimes that had been committed. I always had an answer. Always seemed to know what to say.

Not that they believed me.

CHAPTER 11

Pursuing Sobriety in Ohio

Horrified by reality
*   Consumed by addiction*
My life is based off my own self-affliction

I knew I needed to get off the heroin and alcohol, but had no idea how one accomplished that. Many days had been started with the statement of "I'm not going to get high today; I'm going to go find a job and get my shit together." It never occurred to me that this wasn't an option. Within moments after each time I made this statement, no matter how strong the conviction, I was plotting how I was going to get high ASAP; the circumstances did not matter.

When the thoughts of getting high were in my mind, nothing stopped me from achieving it.

I had a phone conversation one day with my sister, who at the time lived in Ohio with her Christian boyfriend she met off the internet. In that conversation, the idea of me going to Ohio to get sober came up. This really seemed like a million-dollar idea, as I had nowhere to go and was being questioned for several robberies and burglaries. I pulled off a couple of thefts and scrapped the money for a bus ticket. I ended up robbing a couple of kids the night before I left to make sure I could bring some drugs on the bus with me.

Surely this is how you get sober.

My sister set clear rules up for me as far as what it would take for me to be able to stay with her. After a few days, I ran out of the drugs I brought with me. I came up with the idea of going to the doctor's to get some medication for my back. This had worked time and time again and worked on that day as well. I remember returning to my sister's house and walking to the little pizza place to get a snack. Five or six hours later, my sister, her friend, and boyfriend showed up to get me to go back home. I ended up doing nearly all my prescriptions and sitting at the bar drinking myself into a black-out. I don't remember much more of the night.

I woke up the following morning with a return bus ticket back to New Hampshire.

My sister's boyfriend came to pick me up to take me to the bus stop. He filled me in on the night's events. Apparently, I was picking fights at the bar, and when the cops were called, I picked a fight with *them*. My sister called my Opa, and he was able to convince the cops to not take me to jail for who knows what. The cops ended up bringing me to a local hotel. I lucked out again. I still had some pills in my pocket and a buzz that carried over into the morning.

Lord knows I needed the pills due to the shame and remorse I was feeling surrounding the fact that I had just caused a load of grief for my sister. My sister was the one person who has seen every aspect of me. She has stuck by me no matter how screwed up I was, no matter what others said about me, and no matter what I said or did to her.

Here I was, once again shattering the love others shared for me.

CHAPTER 12

Up a River with No Paddle to Row

The choices made that led to this
    When the pitch came with a swing and a miss
Continually making wrong decisions
    Editing my life with improper revisions

When I arrived back in New Hampshire, I called Austin. He filled me in on what I had missed during the week that I was away. Several people were looking for me, including the cops. He stated that it would be best that I go into hiding.

I became homeless for the next twenty-two days. I'd been homeless before, but not knowingly on the run from the police. The worst part was I could not remember what I was wanted for. I remember acting tough with Austin, but I really wanted to curl into a ball and cry.

I stayed in a cemetery that night. I balled up a hoody and used it as a pillow against a headstone. I prayed that night as I looked up to the sky and asked God to take me. Not "take me" like "I offer my life to you" type shit. More along the lines of "If you are real, allow me to not wake up in the morning."

I found myself on the run, an outcast to my family with a stolen cell phone filled with phone numbers of individuals that would not pick up if I called. No one wanted anything to do with me, and rightly

Embrace Your Past Win Your Future | 71

so. I was a scumbag with a raging drug habit that caused me to do things to people that I regretted but had no choice in the matter.

I would stay awake at night, shaming myself for the harm I'd caused others. There is one memory that is burned into my mind. It was July 4 and I had been hiding for well over two weeks. Literally, I hadn't stepped out into the light of day. I had the bright idea to go to my hometown to watch the fireworks display and catch up with a couple of buddies. I managed to get my hands on a written prescription, and so I was walking to the pharmacy to get it filled, completely oblivious to the fact that it was more than likely closed due to it being Independence Day. There I was walking down the busiest section of town as if I were an upstanding citizen.

All of a sudden I heard, "Mark. Mark, what are you doing?" A car pulled up; it was my adoptive mother and stepfather.

"Get in. Let's get some breakfast before you go away," my mother said.

"What do you mean, 'go away'?" I asked.

"You have been on the news for the past two weeks. You are wanted for all kinds of crimes."

At that point, the panic set in and I sprinted away from my mother as fast as I possibly could. Before I knew it, I could hear multiple sirens going. It wasn't my first time running; I was a near veteran at evading. I took to the tree lines so they would have difficulty spotting me. I would periodically peek out to see numerous cruisers driving by. They were everywhere! Did I kill someone? What had I done? A better question: what did they *know* that I had done?

I was terrified in the woods, running for reasons unknown to me.

What I mean by this is that I had done so many things that could have landed me in this situation that it was hard to pinpoint what the police knew I had done. Regardless, I wasn't going to jail tonight. I had plans of getting wasted, and as my experience had shown me up until then, there was nothing that was going to stop that. After a few hours of hiking through the woods, I made it to my friend Phil's house. I walked up to the front door and knocked.

Phil's mother answered. "What are you doing here? Don't you know you are wanted, and a ton of people are looking for you?"

"No, I wasn't aware of that. Is Phil home?"

Phil came downstairs. I begged him to get me stoned, and he did. At the end of our session, he said, "I can't have you coming around here anymore. My mother said she doesn't want the cops here, and they have already come here looking for you."

I headed back to the woods. What was I going to do? Where was I to go? No one wanted me around, and my adoptive mother, my one bail-out plan, had already called the police on me. The feeling was crippling. I managed to steal some alcohol and sat in the woods drinking it. This was the lowest spot I had been in thus far in my life. I had no idea what to do. The only option was to get as loaded as possible in an attempt to forget reality. However, getting loaded is a big challenge when you are hiding in the woods with police from three towns trying to incarcerate you.

I did manage to get drunk that day by walking into stores, taking a couple of pints, and hiding them in my waistband. I had some money, but I surely didn't want to spend it on alcohol. What I wanted was some narcotics; I didn't care what.

It was getting late, and I could hear fireworks going off and laughter and conversation around every turn of the tree line. I had been walking all day, crying and hopeless. In the midst of my pity-party, the thought crossed my mind to go back to Phil's house to see if he left any weed behind that I might be able to steal. I walked back to his house, put a ladder up to his window, and climbed into his bedroom. Sure enough, I found weed and money. I took both and ran back into the woods.

I walked the tree line for a few miles to a ski jump that I had slept at before. I smoked and cried myself to sleep. I had just robbed my one remaining friend.

I woke up to the sound of children. I jumped up, startled and not real clear on what had happened the night before. The children were climbing up the ski jump, collecting firework shells from the night before. I gathered all my belongings (a bag of weed, rolling papers, a lighter, and my cellphone), stuffed it into my pockets, and started to run down the ski jump. The look on the two children's faces is burned into my consciousness. These kids were terrified to see me, but not near as terrified as I was in that moment.

I had been robbing businesses on a daily basis, trying to survive and access substances to release me from the dark thoughts that plagued every waking moment. At this point I was staying in an apartment with some girl I met who knew I was on the run. I had been locked up in her house for twenty days and was only going out at night to rob people and businesses. I was starting to really lose my mind. I was invited to a party a couple of streets down—risky business for someone who had been on the local news and on the front page of newspapers for weeks now.

After the party, a kid I'd met and I decided to break into a couple of stores to see what we could find. While attempting the first burglary, a door opened. I had taken some mushrooms and heroin and was pretty drunk. I was unclear of what time it was, or even where I was. A woman hollered out the door, "I'm calling the cops, you'd better get out of here." So we did.

I told the kid that we needed to stay in the woods so that we wouldn't get caught. He insisted on walking in the road. I knew it was a bad idea, but I was too wasted to argue. The truth is I was tired, not like "I'm ready for bed" or "it's time for a nap" tired. I was tired of living. Everything in me wanted it all to stop.

As soon as we started walking away, the police showed up. They attempted to stop us. The officer knew me by name. In that moment, I made the decision to jump over the guardrail to a twenty-foot fall onto a rock bank and into the Connecticut River. Most people in my position would have never jumped, but I invited the idea of death daily. It was as if I were looking for a way to leave this Earth but didn't have the courage to do it myself.

So I jumped. I landed hard on the rocks below. Smacked my head, rolled my ankle—but that's not even the worst of it. I remember the sobering moment when I was out in the current. I thought my life was over. I couldn't swim; I could barely keep my head above the water. I kicked my shoes and pants off under water to increase buoyancy. My head kept going below the water. It was cold, dark, and moving fast. The undertow kept ripping me below the surface. My mouth filled with water several times. I thought it was over. Finally, some peace and quiet from the daily self-hatred that played in my mind. My head was like a 24/7 infomercial with a really good sales pitch to end it all.

Somehow, I made it to the other side of the river and avoided arrest. Once to the other side of the river, I broke into a house and found clean clothes and shoes that fit, and I was off, back to the apartment complex where I had been hiding out.

After more than twenty days of hiding, I was out of money and drugs again. I had rolled my ankle pretty badly during my river bout, so I decided to seek medical attention.

After being released from the ER, I hobbled on crutches into the parking lot to be met by four or five police cruisers. Before I knew it, guns were drawn, and one of the officers screamed, "If you run, we will shoot you!"

I was on crutches and had just received a shot of fentanyl; I wasn't running anywhere.

The officer who placed handcuffs on me stated that they had been looking for me for quite some time. He also stated, "I will sleep better tonight knowing that a scumbag like you is off the streets."

They booked me at the station and drove me to Sullivan County Jail.

CHAPTER 13

Institutionalized

Now I'm trapped here in prison
I'm accustomed to this cell
And all the wrong decisions
That led me back to this hell

To most people the thought of going to jail is a terrifying realization, but to me it was comforting. I knew that I had a place to sleep and would be fed. When you live a drug-addicted, crime-riddled life such as I had for years, the only concern when in jail is *How long will I be there?* I had engaged in so many criminal activities that it was hard knowing what I was actually being held for.

I remember my first call home. I called my adoptive mother, as I was sure she would be the only person I knew who would answer the phone. I explained to her what had happened and pleaded with her to bail me out.

"Mark, I will not bail you out. I will finally be able to get some sleep knowing that you are safe."

This devastated me. Since early childhood, I identified myself as a victim, so from my point of view, if you had lived the life I lived, you would have surely used drugs and robbed people as well.

In jail I read books, played cards, talked to people about crime, and even gained a few drug connections to use upon leaving. I wrote poetry and sold love poems to other inmates to send to their spouses, pen pals, and family. I only got high a couple times while I was in there, but they kept me on a very high dose of anti-depressants. Even so, I was seriously depressed. Every day, I thought about ending it all. It surely seemed easier than being trapped in my mind.

Wouldn't you have been depressed?

I mean, here I sat in jail after a brutal two-week detox from heroin and alcohol, while sleeping on the floor next to a steel urinal in an eight-by-eight-foot cell with two other inmates. Every day I woke up to the excitement of taking my medication and staring out the window fantasizing about when I would be able to get high again. I had destroyed any and all meaningful relationships in my life and had no one who gave half a fuck about me. Once in a while there would be a fistfight over a honey bun, or who was going to watch what show on television. For some reason, I still experienced pleasure when witnessing someone else's suffering. Somehow it allowed me to shift focus off my own shame and remorse.

I had one role in the eight-man room that I was moved to after detox. My role was that of the "cigarette stasher"—meaning I was in charge of rolling and dispensing cigarettes and hiding them so that if the Correction Officers tossed our room they would not be found. It was a risky game, but I got excited about it. It was similar to feelings I experienced when breaking into a business or robbing a house.

As with any illegal act, the day comes when you get sloppy and get caught. That's exactly what happened. The COs rolled in our room, and right there in the open was a cigarette I was rolling. I received ten days in solitary confinement. If you've ever been in solitary confinement (which most civil humans have not), you know how big of a mind-fuck it can be. I was allowed one pen, one pad of paper, and a Bible. I read the entire Bible while in in my cell and managed to write an entire collection of poems, which I printed and distributed myself a few years later, some of which are used in this book.

The first couple of days in solitary confinement, I was peaceful. I slept fifteen hours per day. I read, drew pictures, wrapped a towel around my face to shield the light that was always on, took night meds and went to sleep. On the third day, I couldn't sleep. I read the Bible and drew and wrote. Over the next several days, I contemplated my entire existence up until that point—which, had you lived the life I had, you can imagine how painful it was. I hated myself, I wanted to die, I couldn't image how I was ever going to build a life for myself. There seemed no hope at all for someone like me.

This ten days of solitude was something that would later have a massive impact on me. I was alone, no communication with the outside world. Unable to sleep due to the light they kept on all day and night. In that ten days I went over my life choices several times. I experienced a lot of self-hatred for my actions. I began to think that there had to be another way. There has to be some other path in life. Was I equal to others who had experienced success and happiness? How does someone like me actually find this?

After the ten days, I was released back into the unit I came from. Everyone was happy to see me, and even more excited that I didn't tell on the cigarette supplier.

I was in county jail for eight months. Toward the end of my stay I started attending recovery meetings in the jail. I really wanted to not have to live a life of getting high and robbing people, but I also had zero interest in feeling the way that I did on a daily basis.

Yet I had no idea how to overcome either of these. When I had my discharge date, the fear and excitement was so strong I could hardly contain myself. The excitement soon wore off when I started to think about all the people who would be coming to collect upon my release. I had burned at least one hundred people. Before I ended up in County, I constantly looked over my shoulders everywhere I went.

I set up a deal with one of my cellmates. He wanted me to meet his girlfriend at a grocery store to drop off some cocaine and cigarettes at the nursing home—what we called the "work-release location"—so that it could be brought back into the jail. This was too good to be true, but I had to check it out. I agreed to do it for him.

For my remaining two days, people in there worshipped me. They asked me a million times a day if I was really going to do it. It's all they talked about. I didn't understand the hype; although I had done it several times, I couldn't stand cocaine. I used drugs and drank alcohol to shut my mind up, not to speed my thoughts up. The last thing I wanted was to be up all night contemplating the crappy hand I had been dealt and how I was destined to die a lonely death.

My adoptive mother and stepfather picked me up from jail the day of my release. They held a huge party for me. Everyone was so hopeful that eight months was what it took for me to turn my life around. I was hopeful as well, but skeptical. I still wanted to die, although I didn't voice that to anyone out of fear I would end up in a psych hospital. I really did want it all to stop.

The following day, I drove twenty miles to meet my probation officer. He stated the ground rules and wished me high hopes. I didn't really hear a word he said. All I could think about was picking up the quarter-ounce of blow and a carton of smokes . . . with zero intentions of dropping it off at the nursing home. Why would I do that? This was the Universe handing me a gift. If you believe in signs, I was certain this was one.

I drove to the grocery store to meet this mystery girl. Sure as shit, she was working in the bakery and waiting for me to arrive. She handed me a decent chunk of cocaine and $50 to buy smokes. I thanked her and headed out of the store. I began obsessing about doing it all. The reality of me hating cocaine was pushed out of my mind by thoughts of how different it would be this time.

I raced back to my mother's house to cook it. Although I didn't like it, I was a wizard at cooking it into rock. First full day out of county jail and I was smoking crack in my mother's house instead of looking for work and getting back on my feet.

On my third night of being home, I was geeking out pretty good when there was a knock on the door. It was a couple of probation officers. They came in my bedroom. They knew I was high. They even asked me if I would pass a urine sample. They didn't lock me back up, which I was surprised about—and which was good, because I probably would have caught a mean ass-whooping from the men who expected me to drop the cocaine off.

They gave me a meeting list of local recovery meetings and stated that I would need to attend a minimum of two per week. I told them that it was the first thing on my to-do list. I sold them tons of sweet promises, which deep down I really wanted to live up to. I had no idea how dark it was going to get for myself, and the people around me.

Later on that week I attended a recovery meeting. It was strange. I didn't feel like I fit in at all, although I knew half of the room. I was more worried about whether or not people I ripped off would come to one of these meetings. I ended up learning that half the room was still getting high and made a couple really good connections. I managed to get some clean time—I'm unsure of exactly how long I had; I think around ninety days. I lied so much I was unsure of what the truth was anymore.

I met a girl at one of the meetings, and she asked me if I could get her some pills. I figured because I was now sober and living a different life I could do it no problem. I scored her a handful of pills from an old buddy. I was going to give them to her at the meeting later on that night.

Nothing ever went the way I planned.

Later that evening, I started getting ready to take a shower. The thought popped into my head: *I bet I could do just one of the pills.* There was no follow-up thought to talk me out of it. Before I knew it, I was high. I didn't end up going to a meeting that night. I went back to get more pills, starting the most vicious run of addiction that I will experience.

From that day forward, I was on a mission to die by means of an overdose. I didn't want to live any longer. This time, I could say I had tried everything. I had even tried the whole recovery-meeting thing. If only people knew how fucked-up those people were, I'm sure the courts wouldn't have sent me there. Or maybe they would have.

For almost a year I did not draw a sober breath.

For my monthly probation visits, I was getting urine detox kits for the first couple of times. After a couple visits, I didn't care anymore. I was hoping they would lock me back up. My dishwashing and prep-cook job was not affording me the opportunity to get as wasted as I needed to on a daily basis. I started stealing money from tables, dipping into the register, and robbing people and businesses at night. I was drinking all day long on top of eating Xanax, smoking copious amounts of weed, and doing heroin. My adoptive mother knew something was up with me, but I don't remember her saying anything to me.

One morning I was getting ready for work—which entailed smoking a joint in my adoptive mom's minivan while drinking a pint. All of a sudden, an unmarked cruiser whipped into my driveway. As soon as I saw it, I knew I was in trouble. It was Dan, my probation officer. In that moment, I remembered that I hadn't checked in with him in a few months, nor had I gone to those dumb recovery meetings or the rehab I was court-ordered to attend. I thought about running, but I didn't feel I was sober enough to get up to the speed necessary to get away. I jumped out of the van and locked the door to it.

"Where have you been?" Dan asked. "I haven't seen you at our scheduled monthly check-ins."

In that moment I experienced something strange, something unidentifiable. Honesty! My mind shot back to that moment of hope in solitary, and I looked him dead in the eyes. "Dan, I can't stay sober. I thought I was going to get high once to dull the voices in my head, but once I started I couldn't stop. There is something wrong with me."

Dan stated that he didn't want to lock me up, but if I wasn't in rehab by next Friday he was going to have to. Dan also explained how him not locking me up that day was a huge risk for him because he could get in trouble for it. I promised him that I would get into treatment by next Friday. I meant it.

I really wanted to go to treatment, to be sober, for the pain to go away. I hated robbing people, walking around with my head to the ground because I didn't want to look anyone in the eyes. I hated constantly lying to my adoptive mother and others who loved me. I absolutely hated not being able to sleep at night even with an expensive buzz, because all the messed-up things I had done and had been done to me would not leave my thoughts.

Although I wanted to fulfill Dan's wishes, I knew there wasn't a chance in hell that I would make it to rehab. I had already made plans to go to a party that night. My brother's tree fort was full of booze and cigarettes I had stolen from a local convenient store I robbed a couple of nights before that I was planning to sell to fund my partying.

I met some people after work and unloaded all my stolen goods into their car to make some money and have resources (drugs) for the party that night. I managed to get some pills, heroin, and even some cocaine. I knew better than to drink liquor with Xanax. That was the combination that always landed me in jail, or at least in a courtroom. Yet none of those thoughts ever came in my mind while in it. No matter how insane of an idea it may have seemed to someone else, I always truly believed that it was going to work out.

My idea that night was that I would party one more night and then go to rehab. I'm pretty sure I even told everyone at the party that I was going to rehab after this party. Regardless of my intentions, what happened was I attempted to steal from the purse of the girl who was driving me home. She threw me out of her jeep in the middle of the road.

I managed to get my hands on a massive crowbar and proceeded to pop the doors of five or six businesses. I filled a backpack with a stack of cash, cigarettes, and Slim Jims.

During my spree, I tripped a silent alarm and was arrested. Well, that was what the court documents later told me. I honestly don't remember most of the evening. What I do remember was waking up a couple days after being placed in Grafton County Jail and asking what in the hell happened. Some of the inmates, who I knew from recovery meetings, filled me in. I was mortified. I was in so much trouble. The judge told me if he saw me again, he was going to send me to prison. Dan was going to be so upset with me.

The next two weeks in County Jail were hell, as the detox from drugs and alcohol took hold, alongside the self-hatred that filled every thought I had.

The thing that they didn't know was that the foundation they gave me as a youth of group homes prepared me for jail and prison. Operating each day based off of a schedule that someone else provided with zero responsibility is easy. Sure, it's not fun, but it's easy. It didn't take long after another brutal detox from drugs and alcohol for me to jump right back into my daily routine. Wake up around noon, eat, play cards, write and draw, watch TV, get night meds, and then read until I fell asleep.

I was constantly calling my court-ordered lawyer and asking if he had any news for me. Each time he would say, "It ain't looking good, kid. They are really trying to send you to prison."

One of the men on my unit suggested I write a letter to this treatment center. It was a year-long rehab and he told me he knew a number of people who got out of going to prison by getting accepted there. I wrote them a letter and sure as shit got accepted. Now I just needed my lawyer to let the court know that everything was all set. I would be going to treatment, so there was no need to pursue a prison sentence.

The court saw things differently.

The day of my sentencing hearing, my lawyer ran up to me with excitement. "They got a sweet deal for you, kid. Two to seven years in prison and successful completion of the rehab you were accepted to."

"I'm not taking that, that's not a deal at all."

"If you don't take it, you're going to do a minimum of ten years."

"Okay, where do I sign?"

After the hearing was over, I headed to New Hampshire State Prison. This happened to be the greatest blessing of my life. Not because they rehabilitated me, but because while incarcerated there, I hit what people in the recovery meetings I attended referred to as a "bottom."

I admit I was a little nervous on the hour ride to the prison. I was in the back of a dark van with several other men. Most of them had been to prison before. We started swapping stories and in no time my fear drifted. Once inside, it was the same thing I had become accustomed to: eat, play cards, write, eat, play cards, sleeping meds, go to bed and do it all over again in the morning. I read and wrote a lot while in there.

My adoptive mother would come a couple of times per month to visit me. She would talk to me about what the family was up to and what she would hope I would be up to upon release.

This time incarceration was different. About two weeks into my sentence, one of my cellmates asked me what kind of medication I was prescribed. I told him I was on Welbutrin, 200mg three times per day. He asked me if I had ever tried sniffing it. I said no, I didn't know that was an option. He shared with me how amazing it was.

That night I dropped my medication down my tucked-in shirt and went back to my bunk. The same man was waiting for me. We sucked the coating off the pill and snorted it. It was the most amazing thing ever. It completely took me out of prison. I did this every day for each med-call. Another man taught me how to catch the pill in my throat and spit it back up once safely back on the unit. This was necessary because of how serious some of the correctional officers took the offense of "cheeking" your medications. I would also sell and trade them for other things.

I smoked weed once while in there. Horrible experience. I got loopy as hell and sat on my bunk and laughed like I was in high school again. The paranoia was too much for me. I didn't do that again. Another time, I got to do some heroin. That was just how I remembered it. Outside of the fact that as soon as you come down you have to frantically begin to pound water to attempt to flush it out of your system to avoid pissing hot and getting a disciplinary hearing. That would only mean time in the hole and less of a chance of getting out on time.

I stayed high the entire time I was in there. Due to the fact that I dropped out of high school, I was mandated to complete my GED before they would release me. That was my one and only accomplishment for the entire two years. I passed my GED. I didn't find out until a few years later how much of an impact that would have on my life.

I pretty much kept to myself in there. I didn't join a gang or get caught up in gambling. Those were two of the cardinal rules a multiple visitor (multi-time inmate) shared with me upon arrival. He said, "Kid, if you want to get out on time, don't get in debt, don't join a gang, and stick to your own." I understood the first two points but had to ask what the third meant. "It means stick with your own color—if it's white, it's right." I followed the first two of the cardinal rules. I talked to anyone, mainly due to the fact that I was high as a kite all the time.

Almost two years into my sentence, I received my letter from the rehab. I opened it in my room as I did with all my mail. You never want to try to read someone's mail in there; I watched multiple fights start because of that. The letter provided me with a date for admission. I had no clue what that meant. Did it mean I was going to get out?

We look forward to your admission on August 23, 2007.

Instantly I was engulfed with fear. That was in two weeks. It was a little after 5:00 p.m., and all I could think about was going to get and sniff my 7:00 p.m. meds. This was it, the bottom, and the absolute lowest imaginable point of my existence. To those of you reading this, it may not seem as bad as some of the other spots I was in earlier in my story, but this was the curtain for me. Someone addicted to drugs and alcohol at the level I was hardly ever reached a circumstantial bottom. I have witnessed countless individuals that have gotten a DWI and sobered up almost instantly.

As you have read throughout my story, the only times I had experienced sober since the beginning of high school was for brief periods when I was physically separated from drugs and alcohol. I didn't sleep that night. I tossed and turned. Every single incident in my life that I regretted flashed through my mind.

I will never make it. I can't even stay sober in prison, how the hell am I going to make it back in the real world?

The following morning, I patiently waited for the yard to open so I could go to the library. I lived there during my free time. I read every book I could get my hands on. Reading took me out of the chaos within my mind. This day just felt different. I had a thought while walking to the library to go to the spirituality section. It happened to be the only section of the library that I had never entered. When I got there, the first book I saw had a man wrapped in an orangish red sheet. This man had the biggest smile on his face that I had ever seen, literally from ear-to-ear. It was a book written by the Dhali Lama. I cannot remember the title of it, but I did read half of it that day.

That night after taking my medication I sat up on my top bunk and wrapped a towel around my head and meditated for the first time. I followed the instructions in the book as best I could. During this period of meditation there were small windows of silence, of stillness. It was just enough to provide me with the hope to carry on the path of seeking. All the other inmates thought it was a joke. They nicknamed me "The Buddha," which, surprisingly, I kind of enjoyed. It sure beat most other nicknames I had been handed throughout the years.

Apparently, the rehab that I was accepted into had the reputation as the hardest treatment center in the country, maybe the world. It was a "therapeutic community." When I asked them to explain, they stated, "You have to tell on each other all day, every day." Telling on people, at least from a convict's point of view, is the worst thing imaginable. There wasn't any lower action that you could engage in. I laughed it all off and tried to forget about it, until the day came.

August 23, 2007. I remember it like it was yesterday.

CHAPTER 14

Liberation of Self

Time will kill a man's mind
Especially in a cell so confined
No chance of freedom, only through prayer
Looking to your corner to find no one is there

I waited impatiently in the processing center of the prison. My adoptive mother and stepfather waited outside to receive me. I was so scared I couldn't sit still. I had this doomy feeling that everything was going to fall apart again, I just didn't know how long it was going to take. I had no one, other than my family, as I had ripped off everyone I had ever come into contact with.

All these thoughts rushed through my mind. I wondered if some of the people I had burned were still looking for me. Was I going to be killed? Many of the individuals I had stolen from had threatened me before coming to prison. Was I going to get high again? Did rehab mean that I was never going to be able to numb the way that I felt inside again? All these thoughts passed the time as the guard processed my paperwork and went through my belongings.

All of a sudden, I heard the guard say, "Crandall #39932, sign here to receive your property, sign here for the terms of your release." After my final signature, the guard popped open the first of three doors. He looked at me. "Good luck, kid. I hope I never see you again, but probably will." I walked forward. I always had something sarcastic to say back to the guards. This day was different. Deep within I knew that his prediction was more than accurate.

How long would it take?

Here it was, the moment I had been waiting two years to see: the sunshine, freedom. It wasn't how I had pictured it at all. I was absolutely terrified. I was so nervous my stomach was inside out. The final gate popped open and my adoptive mother greeted me with a big hug. I don't remember saying much as we drove nearly three hours to the treatment center. I listened to music on my headset that I'd asked my mother to bring for the ride. I did not know what to say. Here were two individuals who have always been there for me no matter what actions I took against them or what hatred spewed from my lips.

I'm sorry! Those words held no meaning coming from me. I had been sorry my whole life, but my actions never backed up remorse. I was sorry. One sorry individual.

When we rolled into the treatment center, I was terrified. I knew that the fear was based on the fact that I had been abusing my medications for the entire two years of my prison sentence, and I had a full prescription in my backpack which I had been obsessing about not turning over to staff upon arrival. I remember skipping med-call that morning, as I wanted this day to actually be the day I got sober. There could have been some effects of not taking my medication enhancing what I was feeling.

My stepfather parked the truck, and we all got out. My old survival instincts kicked in, and I began to act as if I wasn't scared. It was second nature to me. I had shown up to so many places similar to this in the past and found that the only way that I would make it through my sentence was to act as if I was untouchable. To act as if there was nothing wrong with me, and everyone else was fucked up. Not the greatest foundation to begin to build a new life, but you have to start with what you have, and what I had was years and years of walls built up to keep others from getting in. I knew that this way of being had not produced the results that I had always hoped it would, but I knew nothing else.

We walked inside and were met by staff. They all greeted and welcomed me in. I wasn't present to most of the greeting processes as I was still obsessing about sneaking my pills into my room and seeing how many of them I could get up my nose. Staff pulled me into an office and began the intake process. They stated that it was time for me to say goodbye to my adoptive mother and stepfather. With my toughest of tough-guy personas, I said goodbye and went back to the intake process.

My adoptive mother grabbed me by the arm and made a statement that crippled my existence in that moment. She looked me in the eyes. "Mark, you had better do this right, because we are done helping you financially and emotionally. If this doesn't work for you, know that you cannot come home."

I was devastated. I had been plotting how I was going to get back home the entire ride to treatment. What was I going to do now? In that moment, it hit me. This statement was the foundation for a new life. I had no other options. My adoptive father was not going to take me in. Most people in my hometown wanted to hurt me. The curtain had been closed.

In that moment, everything flashed before me.

My adoptive father making the statement that I was a disgrace to his name; my grandmother telling me if I made the news again she was going to disown me. I was hopeless inside. I knew I wasn't going to be able to stay sober, let alone not engage in future criminal activity. It was all I knew up until that point in my life. Regardless of how I was feeling, I had to put my masculine face back on. I couldn't show weakness, or the others in the treatment center would surely attempt to take advantage of me. I may have been clueless on how to stay sober, but institutions were one of my areas of specialty.

We finished the intake process and the staff was about to show me to my room when a strange feeling came over me. I had a thought to give them my medications and explain to them that I couldn't take them any longer. These thoughts were not uncommon for me, or for any humans for that matter, but I rarely listened to them. In this moment, however, I did listen to it. I handed them my medications and explained to them that I wouldn't be taking them, that I had been abusing them for the past two years, and if I was actually going to attempt this thing called sobriety that I had to actually try to be sober. Staff looked at me funny after telling them that I had been snorting my anti-depressants, but took them regardless.

I had heard many people talk about this light that was at the end of the tunnel, but never quite understood the reference until this moment. There was a faint glimmer ahead of me. Unclear to me at the time, but I was about to embark on a life-long quest of transformation. It surely felt strange, to be honest, as I can remember this being only the second time I had done so, but it felt better than the way I had been living.

Treatment consisted of group after group, house meeting after house meeting, outside recovery meetings, meetings at the local church, and what they referred to as Learning Experiences.

These Learning Experiences came about when my peers in the house would call me out on behaviors that were hindering my chances of staying sober and living a productive life. I was like a sitting duck with these things. I was being what they referred to as Confronted by my peers every moment of every day. I was a ticking time bomb. Peers were constantly up my ass, calling me out on swearing, being angry, my facial expressions, and an assortment of other institutionalized behaviors. I was constantly in trouble. I spent a majority of my time in treatment outcasted from my peers. You could find me washing dishes for eight hours at a time, working in the yard, or scrubbing baseboards. They called it "on status."

It may sound miserable, but the methodology of this treatment program was exactly what was needed to beat the shit out of all the belief systems that I had been using to survive up until this point. It took a few months in treatment for me to begin to see that these belief systems were not serving me; they really had caused nothing but struggles for me.

Around six months into treatment I hated everyone. My day consisted of a steady stream of internal dialogue telling me to punch this person, runaway from treatment, get high, and, the most fatal: you are worthless, just end it all. Every day I woke up miserable, hating life and all those around me. I just wanted it all to end. Each night I would lay my head on the pillow and obsess about past mistakes and how hopeless I was. I'm not sure if you ever tried to go to sleep and all you could think about was how everyone who ever said they loved you had walked out of your life, but it's not easy to rest with those thoughts running through your mind. I had thought that treatment was going to be the answer for me, but I felt as if I was in worse shape sober than I was when I was on the run and wasted every moment of my consciousness.

At this point I was going to outside recovery meetings, church two times per week, and nothing was helping me. When I was at church, I would have moments of feeling comfortable in my skin, but as soon as I was back at the treatment facility I wanted to hang myself from a tree. I didn't understand what was wrong with me.

Staff had told me that if I didn't go back on medication they were going to be forced to send me back to prison. I pondered this proposition on several occasions. Surely it would be easier to be back in prison than talk about my fucking feelings and get told on for everything I did wrong. I really didn't want to take medications—I had my whole life, and they never worked. This was the end, the curtain for me.

Suicidal thoughts were becoming more frequent for me. I knew enough to not share these thoughts with anyone, as I would end up in another facility. I was lost. I was crying myself to sleep, wanting the pain to go away. I had always believed that suicide was for quitters, but I could surely empathize with those who took their lives, if they had the screaming in their heads that I did.

There was a group of people who would come to the treatment center every Thursday night to facilitate an in-house recovery meeting. No one ever went to it. This was likely because people in the outside recovery community talked shit about them, saying they were crazy and took recovery a little too seriously. I remember this Thursday night vividly. I had been plotting my last stand. I was going to steal a van from the facility and drive it as fast as it would go into a tree. All day I had been obsessing about these plans. I couldn't see another way out. I had tried everything, and nothing was working. Nothing was providing internal relief for me.

There I stood in the kitchen after dinner one Thursday evening about six months into my stay at treatment, stealing cookies from the walk-in fridge and staring out the back door. These people were standing by their vehicles, smoking cigarettes, drinking coffees, and laughing. I had watched them for weeks wondering what they were on. Surely, people couldn't be that happy *and* be sober. As the curiosity rose in me, a thought came, similar to the one that I'd had when I handed over all my pills during my intake into treatment. The feeling within was that I needed to attend this meeting before it was too late. "Too late" meaning that I was going to end up taking my own life.

As I was walking down to the meeting, I had another thought to say a prayer. Up to that point I thought prayer was some mystical thing that I did not understand. It never worked for me—meaning I never got what I wanted when I asked for it. I said a prayer uncommon to anything I had said before: "God, if you can hear me, please allow me to hear something in this meeting."

I walked into that meeting and there were five or six men and one woman in the room. No one from the treatment center outside of myself was there. I sat down and a man walked over to me and introduced himself. The meeting opened with a prayer and a man spoke for around forty minutes.

What he shared about was nothing I had heard before. This man shared about how he had connected to a power greater than himself and followed direction out of this recovery book and how his whole life was transformed. He spoke with so much confidence and conviction. This man talked about contemplating taking his own life and how he did not see any other viable option to relieve the way he felt inside. Bob was his name.

I felt a glimmer of hope. This man didn't share about all the stuff that he lost and how life had become financially difficult for him. He talked about how he wanted to end his life and saw no end in sight. He made the statement that he went through some twelve-step process, and as a result, slept like a baby. This was all I wanted to hear. I could not remember the last time I got a good night's sleep.

After the meeting was over, I walked up to Bob and made the statement that if he couldn't show me how to feel how he now did, I was going to end my life.

Bob agreed to help me and met me every week before the meeting at my treatment center and talked with me about transformation. He gave me very specific directions, which I followed exactly as he asked. The tasks he gave me were that I needed to start praying and meditating daily, which turned out to be one of the most enlightening directions I had ever received. He also placed emphasis on my need to rectify my past mistakes. I needed to make amends to all who I had stolen from, lied to, cheated on—basically, I needed free myself of all my past regret.

Something began to happen inside of me. I felt hopeful. The light at the end of the tunnel that people used to talk about became visible to me. Weeks rolled by, and Bob and I went deeper and deeper into this transformation work held inside of the twelve steps. Bob became my mentor, my spiritual advisor, and one of my closest friends. He always had an answer for my questions. Usually the opposite of what I was thinking, but I followed his direction closely and began to feel lighter.

Bob guided me through the twelve steps. I know many of you will have something to say about this. I did as well for many years: *Get your God talk out of here. God has no business with a man like me.* Besides, my grandmother told me for years I was going to Hell. In my mind, Hell was surely a greater reality than the life I had been living.

Bob taught me about meditation and prayer, which would be my sword and shield as I navigated my way through this new life. I still didn't think that God wanted anything to do with me; Bob reassured me that I didn't need to believe in God, but needed to be *willing* to believe. I was willing; I had to be, for my only other option was suicide. Drugs and alcohol had stopped providing me with the relief that they once did.

As I went through the twelve-step process, I shared with Bob things I had never shared with anyone. I talked with him about past situations, some of which are outlined in this book and some of which are not. I went all in. I had no choice, as this was the last stop for me. Bob guided me to my first true surrender, a personal inventory, or a fourth step, and into the amends process.

I finished my first fourth step, which was the first opportunity I had at viewing my past outside of the victim mentality that I had been living my entire life. This process is laid out in much more detail in the second half of this book. I finished this quickly, as I was in trouble at my treatment center again and forced to sit at a table for eight hours per day. Things I hadn't thought of in years came up, and I began to see things that I never had before. I began to see all the ways that I had been living and how ineffective they were. Bob showed me some truth about the way I had been living life and the magnitude of my selfishness.

One of the most profound truths for me, and still a distinction that I continue to draw light from, is the extent to which I have played the victim surrounding my past.

Through my years of education, transformation work, and introspection, I have discovered that there is a big difference between *being* a victim and *playing* a victim. I have been a victim of some circumstances that most children do not go through and no child should experience, but I did. This makes me a victim of these circumstances.

Playing the victim, which I had been doing my entire life, is based on me blaming current and past actions on these circumstances.

Bob shared with me that if I wanted to be truly free on the inside, I needed to shed the belief systems surrounding my childhood. This has become a life-long quest for me, and now a focus of much of my professional life to empower individuals to the same truth and freedom I have found.

This is the main reason for writing this book. People have stated for years that I would help millions of people by putting this out into the world. Of course, then I didn't believe, but now I am fully in touch with how powerful the transformation was.

As I carried on with this new quest of self-actualization and empowerment, I began to incorporate spiritual practices into my daily routine. I began to pray and meditate daily and use other tools to gauge my conduct day-to-day. Based upon the way I had been living life before this twelve-step process, it took constant effort for me to be honest and to treat people with love and respect.

I was forced to humble myself and attempt to mend the ways in which I had treated people. This was a terrifying process for me, as many of the amends that I needed to make could land me back in prison. As I was on parole, and if I were to catch a new charge, I would surely go back. Regardless of the potential consequences, I shot out to the world on a quest to repair all the damage that I had caused others. Any consequences that may come as a result of these amends would surely be better than the plan I had formulated before talking with Bob.

I set up a couple of hundred conversations with people who I had come into contact with throughout my life. I sought forgiveness and asked how I might rectify my wrongs. Most of these did not go the way I had intended; many went much more smoothly than I could have ever envisioned. Two examples spring to mind.

I approached Karen to attempt to rectify all the harm I had caused her. She kindly told me I could make it right by never contacting her or her family again. This hurt, but was completely understandable based on the harm I had caused.

The second example is the amends I made to my adoptive father. This wasn't a quick conversation. Every time I went home to visit, I would go see him. I would call to check in on him. This has been a long effort in repairing the damage I caused in his life. Today, he is one of my biggest fans and supporters. He comes to every event I put on, buys and gives away my books, and we talk almost on a weekly basis.

I had started painting and doing drywall work again. This was the only thing I knew up to this point. I quickly found out that I was much more skilled without heroin or alcohol. I was making good money—at least better than all my peers, who were working alongside me in the treatment facility.

Within a few weeks, I had saved enough money to get an apartment and started to obsess about moving out on my own. The only decision that I hadn't made was whether I wanted to move back home to be around my family. I discussed this with Bob, and he recommended that I stay local and carry on with the spiritual path that I had recently been introduced to. A man I became close with in the community was moving out of his apartment and asked me if I was interested in renting it. Obviously, I was; I just wanted to get out of treatment. Nothing could be worse than some of the places that I had slept before.

CHAPTER 15

My New Friend

As I envision what my mind can't shake
Up to this point, my life's been a big mistake
Left with distorted feelings in my head
Every morning I wake I dread

I ended up putting a down-payment on the apartment the day I went to go look at it. Monday morning, I told my counselor Balinda that I was moving out in two weeks. She was upset and scared for me, but my fear had gone away. I was starting to feel happy on a daily basis. Most of my time was spent with other individuals who were attempting to live in the realm of the Spirit. I needed these individuals, as I still had thoughts of robbing and assaulting people.

My new friend God (easier than saying "Higher Power" or "Spirit of the Universe") had other plans for me.

I drove all over the state to talk to others suffering from the same things I had found release from. I was on a mission for increased self-liberation. I found that the more I engaged in these practices, workshops, webinars, and thousands of conversations, the more I recognized that the effect produced was similar to that of drugs or alcohol. All these things made me feel so good inside. The only difference was that the effects of these practices grew stronger, unlike the effects of drugs and alcohol, which decrease the more you use them.

I moved out on my own, and many people who had come into my life donated furniture and other things that I would need. My apartment was near a river. I would sit out on the back porch each morning and listen to the calming sounds of the fast-moving water. Things were going well for me. I was working overtime and saving money. Unfortunately, I didn't anticipate that when it got cold, work would dry up and most painting and drywall companies would lay off their employees until the spring. At the time, I was blind to how dark things were about to get for me.

Work began to slow down as the cold came in. The anniversary of some of the most traumatic moments of my life was approaching. I started to panic; flashes of homelessness and the necessity to resort back to my old lifestyle plagued my daily thoughts. I would get quiet, and these thoughts would drift, and then they would come back even stronger.

Eventually, we were all laid off from work, and I found myself with a couple thousand dollars saved with no work or plan on the horizon. Halloween approached, and I started to think about my biological mother and her birthday. It was also the anniversary of my adoption. I started spending each day doing nothing but thinking about my past. Things got very dark, very quickly. I started reliving all the most traumatic moments of my life.

Here I was, wrapped in fear about my impending homelessness, thinking about all the abuse and neglect of my childhood and isolated from those I had been spending a majority of my time with. Of course, all this was on top of all the harm that I had caused other people throughout my life. I began to experience an extreme depression.

I stopped calling people and spent most of my days watching videos on the internet and writing and reading poetry. Bob suggested that I increase my spiritual practices, which I did. I began to ask God what my next move was to be. I did this day after day. Every time I caught myself in these dark thinking patterns, I would ask what my next move was supposed to be.

It is not my intention to lead you to believe that I was in a constant state of positive thinking. This was one of the darkest times for me. Some days it was a real struggle for me to get out of bed and do anything at all.

Bob called me one evening and asked me if I would fill in for him on a commitment with this man named Jim. Bob made the joke that I should be careful, though—he was gay and might try to fuck me. This was a shock to me, as I knew Jim and did not know he was gay. He did not paint his nails or flip his hair in the wind. He dressed strangely, but I just figured it was because he was an artist. Regardless of his sexuality, I needed to go help someone. I was losing my mind.

Jim picked me up that evening, and we headed to the meeting where we were going to share our experience. The conversation was light on the way there. I remember thinking that homosexuality was contagious. Like he was going to sneeze on me, and I would start wearing leather pants and a pink shirt.

On the way back to my apartment, Jim and I started talking. I had an overwhelming feeling that I should let him know that there would be zero chance of us becoming friends. In that moment, I turned to Jim.

"I just want you to know that I hate faggots."

Jim looked back at me. "Interesting. Let's talk about that."

I shared with him about how I learned of a family member's attraction to men because I snooped on his computer and read through a gay chat site where he was discussing sexual acts with another man. This was a secret I had been holding onto, because if it were known, it could devastate my family.

As Jim and I discussed this, I realized that we were parked in my driveway. We had been talking for a while. Jim and I shifted the conversation to discussing art. I told him of all the poetry I had written and how much I loved art. We made plans to meet up and get lunch and share art with each other.

Jim would become one of my closest friends. To this day, I have a connection with him greater than I have experienced with another man. It is through our friendship that I was able to share this story with you. He told me that "I am an artist and my job is to put my art out into the world. The world gets to determine what it means to them."

CHAPTER 16

Student Loans

Self-esteem is like a maple tree
*   Waiting to be tapped*
Nourish it
*   For it is the sweetest of sap*

A couple months into the practice of asking God in what direction I was to head, I began to start thinking about college. I started to look into schools and areas of study that interested me. I wanted to go to school online due to my lack of self-esteem surrounding my intelligence.

My experience with education was that I didn't do very well at it. Of course, this was mainly due to the influence of drugs and alcohol. I felt as if I should go to school for business, maybe start my own painting and drywall company; this would ensure that I was not laid off during winters. I booked a couple of phone interviews with schools, and after several conversations I narrowed down my choice. When on the phone with the enrollment counselor, she asked me what I wanted to study. I told her that I wanted to study psychology. This baffled me, as I had already made up my mind that I was going to study business. Although I had an overwhelming feeling that I may have made the wrong decision, I went with it.

Turns out, when you take away the drugs and alcohol, I was a pretty intelligent person. My GPA stayed around 4.0. The assignments were easy. I spent that entire winter doing odd jobs and working on psychology homework. Jim approached me about doing some drywall work for him. This job would take me a few days and provide me with the money to pay my rent. I was extremely fearful that I was not going to be able to pay my rent, so I started the same day he showed me what he needed to have done.

When I completed all the work a few days later, I had a thought to steal some money from Jim. The strange thing was that I had money, and he was paying me handsomely for the work I had done. It was not as if I would not be able to eat dinner that night. I took two pockets full of quarters from him. I cannot explain why I did this other than it was another attempt to feed the hole within.

And . . . it did all but that. It was all I could think about. This decision haunted me.

I held onto it for a couple of weeks before I finally called Bob and told him what I had done. He directed me to set up a meeting with Jim and pay him back the money. Bob also questioned me about the amends I was unwilling to make at that time. Could this lack of action be preventing me from overcoming my need to steal from others? This hit me hard, as I did not want to make amends with those I had harmed in my past. I had six burglary amends and two robbery amends left to make. I was not convicted for these, but if convicted, I would be a career criminal and face a minimum of seven to fifteen years in prison.

Although I had applied the practices of "telling on myself" and "asking forgiveness for my sins," I still felt horrible about what I had done. I've always been extremely judgmental of myself, but it seemed to intensify when sober. Maybe it had always been as intense; I just didn't realize it as much, due to the fact that I was minimizing my consciousness through substance abuse. I hated myself for the fact that I had hurt another person who I cared about.

What was wrong with me? Would I ever be normal?

I reached out to Jim and asked if he would be willing to get dinner with me that night. He agreed, and we met up. I was terrified, due to the fact that I had never owned up to stealing unless I was caught. I pulled $40 out of my pocket and handed it to him; I explained what I had done and asked if there was anything else I could do to make this right. He was very receptive and stated that he forgave me and didn't view me any differently.

He may not have, but *I* sure did. I was a thief. Always had been and would probably never change. You know the old saying: "once a thief, always a thief."

CHAPTER 17

Redemption

Freedom's at my fingertips once and for all
     Never again for this addiction will I crawl
As another day passes me by
     Just for today, I see no reason to die

A couple weeks after my attempt at rectifying yet another mistake, I decided to set up a meeting with my parole officer. I had been guided to tell him about stealing from Jim and how I needed to make amends back home, and to seek his guidance on how to navigate this without ending up back in prison. I set up an appointment for the following morning.

I spent that entire day and night obsessing about how he was going to send me back to prison. I had stolen, and was about to confess to a bunch of crimes; why would he *not* send me back?

When I walked in, he told me to sit down, and so I did.

"What's this all about?"

I told him everything. I poured it out as quick as I could, because I figured my willingness to be honest had a shelf life.

He kicked his feet up on his desk. "Mark, if you are arrested for any of these, I will make sure you don't see another day in prison. You, my friend, are ready to get off parole. I will submit the paperwork for early termination."

I headed home that weekend and made ten amends. As I made more of these, my self-hatred began to vanish. I wasn't looking over my shoulder as much. I started to see that there was another way for me to live life. The ten days that I spent in solitary confinement were coming full circle. My contemplations and wishes were coming true. I was on fire. My depressive thoughts were gone. I had purpose. I was on a mission to help people and discover more and more internal freedom.

A few weeks later, my paperwork came in the mail stating that I had been released from parole three and a half years early due to good behavior. I could not believe it! Why had I not experienced this amazing life the several other times I wanted to stop getting high and drunk? That did not matter. Now was my time, and I needed to continue to seek God's will, for this new life was a direct result of seeking more and more of this spiritual life.

Thoughts of moving to a bigger area with more opportunity came into my meditation practice for a few weeks straight, so I decided to take some action and see if there was any validity to it. I followed through and started reaching out to friends to see if they had rooms for rent. After some time, I moved to the Sea Coast and around the same time enrolled into a university to finish out my undergraduate degree.

After moving, I quickly and easily obtained a position on a painting crew, making good money. I began to save all my earnings outside of what I needed to live. I was tired of living paycheck to paycheck. It became an obsession to see how much money I could save. My Oma used to tell me that I needed to have six months of all my expenses put away because you never knew what life was going to hand you. In the back of my mind, every dollar I didn't have saved meant I was much closer to being homeless again.

It didn't take me long to become engulfed in the recovery community on the Sea Coast. I made many friends, some of whom I still have today. One of these friends wanted me to attend a young people's recovery conference in New York with her and some other people. I wasn't excited about this invite due to how socially awkward I could still sometimes be. I didn't want to go and told her this. She insisted that I go, and so I did.

It was absolute chaos at this conference. People were screaming and banging on drums. Total shenanigans! After making our way through the hotel to our room, I calmed down.

In the hotel room, a good friend of mine and I decided to meditate to ground ourselves. As we were meditating, the door opened. There were three women who stated they were going to be staying in the hotel room with us. One of these women was the most beautiful person I had ever set my eyes upon. We stared at each other for a moment, and then they walked out of the room, and my friend and I continued to meditate.

As the conference rolled on, I began to have fun. I was hanging out and talking with people and letting my hair down.

The first night of the conference, I ended up sleeping in the same bed as the woman I had a moment with in the hotel room earlier that day. (This may sound romantic, but there was, like, twelve people staying in that hotel room, three or four of whom were in each bed in the room.) That woman's name was Megan, and we laid next to each other and talked that evening and even cuddled a bit.

We didn't talk after that until the following evening. I searched for her all day. There was a pit in my stomach that I hadn't felt since Karen dumped me back in high school. I hated this feeling. It reminded me of all those times my biological mother would state that she was coming to visit and then never showed up.

I came to find out that Megan had driven from New York back to Pennsylvania for a funeral. She returned late that evening. I was sitting in the main room in which the big recovery meeting was to be held. She walked in with her other two friends. She was gorgeous. My heart melted, and I became giddy with joy. She sat next to me and we talked. After the meeting, we decided to walk around New York City. We talked and walked for hours and hours. I stole a few kisses, and we held hands as we walked.

The moment that changed me forever was when a homeless man asked us for money. I sat down next to him on the dirty sidewalk and talked with him. Megan sat down next to me without hesitation. I fell in love. We stayed up all night together. We exchanged phone numbers and have not stopped being together and growing spiritually since that night.

A few months later, I moved in with Megan and we started to build our lives together. We hardly ever fought; when we did have disagreements, they were short-lived and usually ended with us laughing at each other.

Shortly after moving in with Megan, I started my final classes of my undergraduate degree. I started to seek positions in the field of Human Services in which I had been studying. It was a terrifying process due to the extensive criminal background that I had accrued as a result of my drug addiction and alcoholism. I was facing extreme difficulty even finding an agency that would allow me to come in and interview. I had no practical experience working in the field of human services. The only thing that I had working for me was my knowledge and experiences of "living on the dark side." I later found—and this is still continually revealed to me—how beneficial all of my darkest experiences are in the light of empowering others to change.

The first couple weeks in my final classes, it was suggested that I find a mentor, someone to help guide me in the field. One of my professors had intrigued me. Here was a man with an overwhelming personality, so much confidence and intelligence. I walked up to him on one of the breaks and asked him to guide me, to help me make my way. His name was Marvin. He asked me several questions and then told me to meet him for lunch, and so I did. This man called a friend of his and asked if she would interview me for a position working with runaway and homeless youth. She agreed to interview me, and I nailed it. During the interview, I tapped into skills I was unaware of at the time and started interviewing the youth that was there to interview me. I was hired for the position, and, although I didn't know it at the time, my entire life was about to change forever.

The job that I was hired for allowed me to work with runaway and homeless youth in a drop-in center. The first year at this job was fun, difficult, and brought up all my childhood traumas. I would often go home so distraught that I didn't know if I would be able to go to work the following day. I continued to practice meditation and other introspection/transformational work which allowed me to overcome these blocks and go further and further as a professional and a spiritual being.

I've spent much of my life not being able to fall asleep at night. Due to the realm of the Spirit that Bob introduced me to, I now sleep soundly at night. I currently have no one I knowingly owe amends to. I don't owe anyone money due to having made hundreds of amends to people and businesses I had stolen from.

Marvin stayed a mentor of mine for years. He became a huge influence on my professional and spiritual life. After two years, I decided to seek new employment. I wanted to work at the youth detention center but knew they would never hire a felon. I applied anyway, as the power of God had smashed my beliefs before by creating possibility in the wake of self-judgment, so why not now?

I applied and was hired. One of very few felons hired by the state.

The grass was not greener on the other side of the fence, however. I hated working there. Having lived in similar institutions as a youth, I was unable to separate myself enough from my empathy for the youth. My difficulties were intensified by the fact that the gossip spread surrounding my criminal past. Some of my coworkers were supportive of me; others avoided me. Someone even went so far as to notify the local newspaper and tell them that I had been hired. They wrote an article about how the state had hired a convict to oversee youth.

Some of my coworkers felt as if this should have bothered me more than it did. I viewed this as God showing others what He had led me to walk through as a pure demonstration of His power. To me, this was a huge demonstration of the power of spiritual practices.

CHAPTER 18

Marriage

I thought it was the end
*   Then I felt you by my side*
With you in my corner
*   Never again will I hide*

Megan and I had been together for about one and a half years, and I knew it was nearing time to ask her to marry me. I was pretty resistant to marriage, as I had seen very few—if any—last for life as most all wedding vows state.

I sought the counsel of one of the pastors of a church where one of my recovery meetings was hosted. I also had a new spiritual advisor. His name was Brian, and he had been married for years and had a couple of children. He navigated his relationship with so much love and grace; I prayed that I could someday have something that beautiful. I had countless conversations regarding marrying Megan. I decided it was time. I was never in a million years going to find another woman as strong, passionate, and beautiful as the one I had. I asked both of her fathers (her biological father and her mother's new husband) for their permission to marry her. They both gave me their blessings, and her mother even sent me a set of rings she had if I wanted to use them. I was so terrified that as soon as the rings arrived in the mail, I opened the package and proposed. I was supposed to wait and do it in Aruba on a family trip, but I just could not wait.

We were married on September 8, 2012—one of the greatest days of my life.

I graduated from the University of New Hampshire with a master's degree in Social Work (MSW). I was planning to take the easier route of obtaining my degree through an easier program, but Marvin insisted that I was smart enough to obtain my MSW. This three-year program was one of the most difficult tasks I engaged in since entering recovery. Both of my adoptive parents were in attendance at the graduation ceremony. The relationships that I have with them today are amazing. I know that if my life had taken a different turn, I would not be the strong man that I am today.

Megan and I ended up moving to Austin, Texas, several years later in an attempt to avoid winter. Well, we *thought* it was to avoid winter; God always has a plan, even if I'm unaware of His workings at the time. Since arriving, we have witnessed nothing but the most amazing opportunities. My life is more beautiful than I could have ever imagined.

On August 23, 2007—the day I walked out of New Hampshire State Prison—the fear that I experienced would be the fuel with which I would rebuild my life. I have done and continue to do work each and every day to break away from the life I once lived.

The greatest distinction that I have found throughout all the introspection work that I have done is that there is a difference between being a victim and playing one. I have stopped playing the victim. In the next section of this book, I'm going to share with you how I was able to stop playing the victim and how I guide others through the practices and exercises so that they may find the freedom I have found.

As a result of moving to Austin, I have been placed in the paths of some brilliantly motivating individuals. I have embarked on a quest that God put on my heart at eighteen years old to become an author, motivational speaker, and transformational coach. I've started my business of coaching individuals to overcome their limiting beliefs and begin to live truly powerful lives. The more coaching, speaking, and entrepreneurial endeavors I indulge in, the more I tap into my true power. My business has flourished and, as a result, has laid the groundwork for me to empower countless individuals.

Who would have thought that all my mistakes and misfortunes would one day develop into the foundation of helping others live more fulfilling lives?

As a result of my guidance to devote my life to helping others, I have had some amazing conversations surrounding the possibility of transforming self-hatred into love, increasing the success of their businesses, discovering and following their true callings.

My experience has been that most people spend their lives trapped in "would've, could've, should've." I've devoted my life's work to ending regret and accomplishing everything there is to accomplish in this life. I hope that my story inspires you to tap into your true potential and not allow situations from your past, any limiting belief, or any self-judgment, stop you from fully living in that potential.

The guiding force in devoting my time to writing this book was the possibility of it touching the lives of millions of individuals who believe that their past will dictate their future. This has not been the case for me thus far in life, and I sincerely hope it is not so for you. I am grateful for all the darkest points of my life; each of these have allowed me the opportunity for spiritual growth. I will end this story with something I say often:

"Failure" is a word reserved for those who have quit.

Although this story has come to an end, this is really a beginning. In Part 2, I will share with you how I transformed my life and have become devoted to empowering others to transform theirs as well. Over the past ten-plus years, I have tapped into the power that is stored within spiritual practices and transformation work, and I want more and more of it. I have created the possibility of my trials and tribulations touching the lives of millions of people and empowering them to take the actions necessary to transform their own lives.

If there is one thing that has become extremely clear to me, it is that we are not promised tomorrow. This exact moment is all we have. Yet I spent most of my life on layaway—meaning, I'm always putting things off as if I'm promised the opportunity to complete them at a later time.

Procrastination is nothing more than the delusion that tomorrow is promised.
—*Mark Crandall, LMSW, LCDC*

PART II:

The difference between *being* a victim and *playing* a victim.

Introduction to Part II

When I was nearing the end of the launch of Part I of this book, *Eulogy of Childhood Memories*, there was a great urgency to release it. It wasn't complete—I knew that. But I held so much fear associated with the actual release that I felt I needed to put it out into the world ASAP before I changed my mind. So I did.

Well . . . now the time has come to complete what I started.

This section is a step-by-step guide to how I turned my self-hatred, routed in my past trauma and transgressions, into the greatest resource I possess to create an epic life of unstoppable potential—and how you can, too.

This section is of extreme importance to the world.

Today, most of us are unable to see the difference between *being* a victim and *playing* one.

This is partly due to the fact that society is structured to support *playing the victim*. The most unfortunate part of this is that most of us spend our lives viewing the world through the lens of stories we make up based off past experiences.

In this writing I will discuss the stories that *I* formulated and how these shaped my fate in the world. I will also discuss my own process through the transformation of these thoughts, which produced a revolutionary shift in my outlook on myself and the world.

The process I'm going to outline will allow you, the reader, to stop viewing your past as a liability and begin viewing it as your greatest asset. If you have always been a victim of circumstances beyond your control, I would urge you to open your mind and be willing to view these experiences through a new scope.

If you do not relate to the statement I just made, well, I also encourage you to read on, as the exercises I lay out can lead anyone to a liberation free from self-judging thoughts.

This distinction—the difference between being a victim and playing one—absolutely revolutionized my life.

As recounted in Part I of this book, I was the victim of many misfortunes throughout my childhood. My biological parents separated before I was old enough to know what that meant. My mother was addicted to cocaine; dated men who mistreated me, handcuffed me, and locked me in a closet; and forfeited her rights as a parent. As a result, my sister and I were removed by the state. We were both placed into the same foster home. On multiple occasions my biological parents stated they were going to come and see us and did not. All of this stuff happened **<u>to us</u>**.

Do you see how "to us" is in bold and underlined?

This is purposeful. I want to highlight that this is the type of language that has kept me trapped in a victim mentality for years.

I do not share all of this with you in an attempt to try and elicit empathy, or to get you to feel bad for me.

This has been laid out to set the groundwork for what it truly means to be a "victim." You see, I *am* a victim of all of the situations throughout my life that were outlined in detail in the first part of this book. I spent many years, without even knowing it, justifying my thoughts and actions based off these past situations. I was in the "victim" mentality, but at the time I couldn't see that anything was wrong, as I had been living within this mind state for so long.

Now I can see that living from the standpoint of *playing the victim* has caused me much heartache, disappointment, and resentment, and limits what I believe and do not believe I can achieve.

Playing the victim hindered my life's potential and limited my opinion of myself. While in the victim mindset it was impossible for me to see the magnitude to which it was affecting me. My greatest awakening thus far on the path of transformation was when I saw that my entire life had been determined from the mindset of a victim. This shook me to my core. When I truly evaluated various circumstances in my life and saw the truth—*I was making decisions for my future based on my past*—I swallowed hard.

When I walk coaching clients through some of the exercises in this book, they go through a similar awakening. Often times, we spend multiple coaching sessions evaluating their past and the decisions that were made in those moments. Once you have done this thoroughly, and honestly, you too will have some insight into what it means to play the victim.

Throughout this book I will use many experiences, most of which are from my childhood, which could be viewed as me being a victim. A victim of circumstances. I would ask that you place yourself into your own circumstances and evaluate your own potential "playing the victim" belief systems.

The situations that happened to you DO NOT need to match up with my own. I'm merely using mine as examples in an attempt to draw out your own experiences. As we continue down this path, please keep in mind that by comparing yourself to me with statements like "That didn't happen to me" or "He doesn't understand," you are currently in the midst of the victim mentality.

However, if you keep an open mind throughout your reading of this book, you will witness the mental shift I underwent to change my perspective from "All of these things happened *to* me" to "All of these things happened *for* me."

My promise to you is that you *can* break free from the dark shadows of a subconscious need to play the victim. In this part of the book I will outline a detailed plan of action which will empower anyone to overcome their past and to instead begin to use their past as fuel to motivate the actions necessary to live an extraordinary life.

The separation and identification of *this happened **to** me* to *this happened for me* holds the key to the future of countless people leading epic lives. I will share how I broke free from blaming, resentment, sadness, self-doubt, and judgment and entered a position of viewing all of the things that have happened for me thus far in life as *assets*.

Yes, I said assets.

I will teach you the tools I used to turn what used to be the biggest barriers in my life into the greatest resources I possess.

Trust me.

If I can break free from a victim mentality, so can you.

Are you ready to shed some light and open the doors to endless possibilities?

CHAPTER 1

I'm a Victim

Many of you, I'm sure, have read Part I of this book, *Eulogy of Childhood Memories*. In it I discuss at length some of the situations that took place throughout my childhood and into my teenage years. I'm going to summarize a few of the lasting memories here, now, to provide some context for you. This will be crucial for when I outline the plan of action I utilized to break free from letting my past control my future.

In *Eulogy of Childhood Memories*, I talk briefly about how I used my past experiences to shield myself from the world, but I do not go into the detail that I wish to now as to how these belief systems actually shielded me from my true potential. Together we will break down the shield that you yourself have lived behind for years.

As I share my examples, I will provide stopping points for reflection. In these stopping points, my challenge to you is to begin to evaluate your own life. Where have you been trapped in similar thought patterns? Where have you been stopped?

As I said in the introduction to Part II, I urge you to not minimize or magnify your experiences compared to mine. When you are in the victim role, the depth of the situation matters little in comparison to the limits that the victim role places on your life.

Before we begin to challenge your thoughts and beliefs, however, let me re-share some of my own experiences with playing the victim.

The first example that I am going to use I believe is the springboard to which I built a structure of victimhood around my life. When I was six or seven years old, my sister and I went to have a "visitation" with my biological mother. Christmas was nearing, and as you can imagine, the excitement was roaring within us. I was a selfish child in constant thought of what I could get from the world, and Christmas was an epic platform to allow my selfishness to roar. Little did I know that this visitation was going to become a springboard in which I would launch out into countless years of victimhood.

The details of the visit are still hazy to this day, though one situation is burned into my brain. I remember my biological mother had purchased some gifts for my sister and me. They were under her tree in her apartment in which we were visiting. One gift in particular stood out to me. She had purchased us those big plastic candy canes filled with Christmas candy. As a child, I loved sweets. In that moment, something happened to my brain when I knew I was about to eat them; I wanted them but was told that I could not have them.

As the story goes, I was begging my biological mother for the candy she had purchased for us. I'm sure I was being absolutely obnoxious at the time, as I often was. The result of my biological mother's frustration ended with me being screamed at and then handcuffed and locked in her kitchen closet. This may have been done with playful intentions, although that was not what registered in my mind. What rang through my brain then, and for some years to follow, was the deepest terror I had and currently have ever experienced. My breath was constricted; it was dark; I could hear my biological mother screaming at me from her kitchen.

In that moment my entire life changed. Even today, if I share with anyone that I was handcuffed and locked in a closet as a child, I'm careful to NOT set the stage for me to crawl back into the victim mentality that I just outlined. For years, the response from others has allowed me to play the victim.

People have said, "You poor baby," "You were just a child," "You only wanted candy!" "What was wrong with your mother?" "No one should have that happen to them!" All of those statements are true, of course. It was unfortunate, and no child should have to go through such an experience.

But . . . it *did* happen.

There is one main problem with living in "victim" situations for too long. As humans, we start to intensify the story of what happened.

Yes, I said it. We start to *lie* about what happened. We begin to make up and increase the drama of what actually happened.

I know, I know.

Many of you, while reading this, will have the urge to "play the victim" about what I just said. If you approach the distinction that I am about to share with an open mind, however, then you yourself can go from victim to VICTOR!

That's right.

With an open mind, you can break free of the story that has plagued you. The stories that have left you feeling purposeless or living with darkness in your soul are about to be broken wide open and become the fuel to shoot you off like a rocket.

My Story

The more I shared this story and embellished it, the more I withdrew from life. I used this story as a means of getting people to feel bad for me. I used it to get out of troubling situations in which I placed myself. In short, I used this story from my past to limit my own potential in the future.

Within the situation that I outlined, I wove in a multitude of other thoughts, feelings, emotions, and even manipulated the actual storyline.

Why? you may be asking.

Because once I began sharing it with others, the effect the story produced internally, inside of me, began to diminish. I needed to add more intensified highlights. I wanted people to see it as more than it actually was. I wanted people to feel more sympathetic toward me.

As the years went on, my story continually compounded. In simple terms, I made things up. I began sharing the backstory of my biological mother's addiction. I wanted to set the stage of cocaine in lines all over her kitchen table. I would outline how I was crying in the closet, contemplating my own existence.

Suicidal at age six or seven? I think not! I just wanted Christmas candy. But the more I shared it, the more I added to it. The older I got, the more highlights I would add.

In reality, my mother's boyfriend placed me in handcuffs and I spent a period of time in the closet with them on.

But the story *became* that I was handcuffed and locked in a closet, and my biological mother did this while fueled up on booze and cocaine, and I was crying and being screamed at, and I was called a host of names, and all sorts of mean and degrading things filled the walls of that closet, and while in the closet I started having thoughts of ending my life, and I was beaten while in the closet and eventually rescued by my adoptive parents, not hours, but *days* later.

I told myself I was unlovable, unworthy of any good from this life. I will outline this further in a couple of pages. When I do, it is my hope that you have an "A-ha!" moment of your own. You will come to see that most humans on Earth have been living their lives within a story they tell themselves and others. Most humans play the victim on a daily basis without even recognizing that they are doing so.

Do you see what we do to maintain the illusion that we're victims?

The first sentence of the above elaborated example is true; the rest that follows was compounded upon as a result of playing the victim for so many years. The separation of what actually happened and what I make up to defend my role of the victim has set me free of my need to play the victim.

Later on, I will outline an exercise that anyone can undergo and become free of the hindrances that come from playing the victim. I just wanted you to see the process of what we do as humans for the sake of "protecting ourselves."

Why Play the Victim?

People play the victim in their lives because there is a great internal payoff that comes from the masks they wear. This means that there is some internal pleasure or confirmation that takes place when they assume the role they have built up throughout the years. When we begin to evaluate the roles we have created and played, and really bring to light the depths in which these roles have hindered our growth, connection, inner peace, and so much more, we begin to find the strength and ambition to move past the need to play the victim.

The victim role that I played for years was a manifestation of lies I had attached to the situation that took place, which did in fact involve me handcuffed in a closet—again, that's what really, truly happened. I found, however, that the more I shared this story with others the less power it held for me. Meaning, the response I received from others did not create the emotional response that I craved in order to feel validated.

When I started sharing this situation, people would say "You poor child," "No one should be treated that way," "You're so strong for sharing that with the world!" But the more I heard these things from others, the less and less I would receive the once-powerful effect produced.

The payoff for the share was not as intense as it once was. As a way of intensifying the response from others, I realized, I had to intensify the story. And sure enough, by adding little embellishments to my story, the response I received from others became stronger and stronger.

Let me explain what I mean by the "response I received." This does not necessarily mean that they started crying or that they demanded to hold me in their arms and pat my head while telling me it was going to be okay. The responses I am suggesting are when others co-sign the story. What I mean by *co-sign* is that others agree with your perspective. Meaning, they *allow you to play the victim*. But the more I shared the story, the less and less I really felt validated in playing my victim role. So by intensifying the story I learned that people would intensify their thoughts and feelings surrounding what had happened to me.

Why lie?

The payoff, that's why!

Without knowing it at the time, I was embellishing the story so that people would experience shock and awe. I had worked this whole thing up in my own head to the point that I needed hugs, or tears, or a recognition that I was a miracle. If I received all of the above, then I knew I had really put my mask on perfectly that day.

The feelings that I experienced needed to be stronger than the cost of living in the victim role, which together we are about to dissect.

When playing the victim role, the payoff needs to be much greater than what it is internally and externally costing me. But looking back on it now, the payoff never outweighed what it actually cost me. The delusion of security and confirmation kept me from truly identifying and evaluating the situation enough to step out of the shadows, so to speak. In the end, the role of playing the victim is a never-ending circle of lies compounded by internal suffering and the inability to break free and become the powerful human that everyone has the capability of becoming.

My payoff was so loaded when I first took a look at it and accepted it, that it actually created some intense emotion within. The story that I had built up surrounding the situation that I have outlined allowed me to be content living a very small life.

Payoff:

- Did not need to take action on anything, because I wasn't worth anything great anyway.

- Did not need to put any effort into relationships, because they would leave and/or hurt me.

- No need to educate myself, because I was stupid and would never be able to make use of it.

- Allowed myself the ability to hold ZERO expectations for how I was living my life.

These four main points are the main reasons that I continued to elaborate on my own story. But when you shine light on the payoff versus the cost, it makes little to no sense. Here's the main problem with playing the victim role:

Most people—myself included—are unable to see that we are playing the victim. It becomes who we are internally and externally. We become so lost in the story and reaping what we believe to be rewards within the payoff that the possibility of breaking free does not come into our consciousness. It's very hard to identify a problem when you cannot see one.

Humans usually only identify something as a problem when there is a block placed in front of them. This means that there is a situation that is presented that causes them severe emotional pain. If you have been playing the victim as I was for years, and experiencing the emotional pain for that long, it will be nearly impossible to see it for what it truly is.

This becomes a barrier, holding you back from living the life of your wildest dreams.

The only way I have found to "snap out of it" is to constructively evaluate what playing the victim is actually costing you. When you view the cost versus the payoff, you will be much more willing to take the necessary actions to step out from behind your mask. If you have the experience I had almost twelve years ago, you will smash your mask—"smashing my mask" being a metaphor for devoting my life to transformational work and sharing my findings with the world.

Is the Cost Worth It?

Throughout the years that I wore the victim mask, I truly believed that it was serving me. I believed that the role I had created was who I actually was. It was not until 2007, when I began doing some extreme introspective work, that I slowly began to realize that it was not serving me at all.

In fact, it had been costing me EVERYTHING.

All my hopes and dreams were hiding behind this one situation. This one situation had literally dictated the direction of my entire life. The stories that I created about this situation had cost me more than I could have ever imagined.

Since I was sixteen years old, I wanted to be an author and speaker. Due to the story that I had built up about this closet incident (and several others), I could never get out of my own way to take any forward action. Every time I attempted to start taking action, a self-defeating thought would come in and stop me dead in my tracks.

You know the thoughts:

What if I fail?

What if they find out who I am?

Blah blah blah. These thoughts go on and on—and have so frequently over the years that I generally don't even identify them when they crop up. They literally became a working part of my mind.

What It Cost Me

Keep in mind that your identification of the actual cost may not be as defined as mine. This is not a bad thing at all. In the realm of transformation, everyone has a starting point—and the best part about the realm of transformation is that there is no end point. So, wherever this finds you is exactly where it is supposed to find you.

The cost of living in this victim role led me to a life of drug addiction, criminal offenses, and distraught relationships; I was broke, homeless, uneducated, unemployable, and angry, and I blamed it all on the world around me.

It cost me peace of mind. I was always on edge and never content with anything I had; I was in a constant search for something more, although nothing actually filled me up.

This cost me healthy relationships. I pushed people away under the excuse that no one was ever going to hurt me again like my mother had. I took my resentment out on other women in my life in an attempt to try and get revenge for what my mother had done to me.

It cost me self-confidence as well. I never took action on my hopes or dreams. I never sought to better my situation in life, because in my mind I was unworthy, and no one would listen or want to hear what I offered anyway.

It also cost me financial security. I was never focused on saving my money or even paying my bills, because I needed to obtain things that would provide me with momentary relief; but that fleeting validation never did what I wanted it to—no matter how much I spent, it never made me feel as if I had or was enough.

It cost me emotional connection. My intimate relationships were always very shallow because I told myself that if I provided too much insight into who I actually was, it would be used against me.

This also allowed me to justify running away. If I felt like a relationship was getting too close to the surface (or the relationship was no longer allowing me to live inside of my victim role), then I would get out and seek another that would provide the relief I needed.

So as you read through these, could you justify that they outweigh the payoff?

No?

Neither could I. Not when I honestly evaluated them.

When you shine direct light on the situation, removing your story from it, the cost never outweighs the payoff. Yet, most people never break free from their story. As a result, they continue to live their lives sheltered, afraid, and constricted.

The situation is the situation. Meaning, DO NOT compare yours to mine. In the realm of victim playing, there is no rating system on the situation in which we placed our story. If you have attached a story to it and it has hindered all aspects of your life, then it is large enough to evaluate and break free from. Don't you think?

I have taken so many situations throughout my life and run them through this exercise. I guarantee that the cost was never greater than the payoff I received.

Are you ready to begin the journey of transformation, or to further where you currently are?

Are you ready to smash through the barriers preventing you from living the life of your dreams?

Are you ready to become truly unstoppable in all areas of your life?

If you answered YES to any of these questions, then you are beginning to see the weight of staying where you are in life. You see how small you are playing in this world. For years, I just tried to stay in my own lane and not ripple the waters, so to speak.

Now . . . I'm out to create massive waves!

Time to grab a notebook and a pen and begin to shine a flashlight into the darkness of your mind. On a piece of paper, write these headings, separating each heading by about ten lines:

1. What happened? (facts without any additions; the specific details)
2. How have I compounded what actually happened? (embellishments you added to #1)
3. What is the reward? (the payoff)
4. How is it limiting my true potential? ("true potential" being the result of breaking free from playing the victim)

Examples from what I have shared with you already:

1. **What happened?:** My mother's boyfriend handcuffed me and locked me in the closet for a period of time, ignoring my screams. (Remember, we are getting as specific as we possibly can. We want to separate what actually happened from all that we have added.)
2. **How have I compounded what actually happened?:** Write out all additions that you have placed on the truth. These are thoughts/feelings, exaggerations, belief systems, placing blame, self-judgments, etc.—anything at all that you have added to the specifics of what actually happened.

3. **What is the reward?**: This is all the ways you have been rewarded by living in your own elaborated story. (Example: *I have an excuse to be lazy, I justify terminating relationships*, etc.)

4. **How is it limiting my true potential?**: These are all the internal and external consequences from continuing to live behind your story that you have created surrounding what actually happened to you. (Example: *I lack true connection, I lack purpose, I'm easily angered*, etc.)

Now that you have taken a look at various situations throughout your life more thoroughly than you probably had before, how are you feeling?

The exercise you have engaged in is not new at all. Countless transformation practices use variations of the same exercise to break free from situations. It is my hope that I make this much more tangible for those who read this book and use the above exercise.

It is not uncommon to feel worse internally than before you started the exercise. Especially if you are anything like me: I had been living within countless lies for years and years. When I first started to engage in introspective work, it was indeed very uncomfortable.

Why is it so uncomfortable?

Picture that you are building a home. You go through all the stages of building a home: you hire a contractor to write the blue prints; the contractor hires all the companies to lay the foundation, frame the house, build the house, and paint it. Finally, you move in and put your touch on it. You add all sorts of trinkets to the inside and out.

You live in this house for years. There is a slow leak in the attic that you are unaware of. The water is causing damage that you cannot see. The longer the leak goes unchecked, the more damage is created. You decide to have some work done on your roof, and when the roofer does their initial inspection, they find the leak and report it back to you. The roofer tells you that in order to fix the problem, you have to completely take your house apart. The roofer states that the only way to find out exactly what is wrong is to dismantle your house piece-by-piece and inspect each piece of material that was originally used to build your house.

So, after this exercise, you are now looking over a dismantled house. You can either stress over the fact that you have a dismantled house or put that energy into building a better house than you had before. Or you can carry on with your life pretending that nothing is wrong internally.

What is your choice?

I recommend that instead of stressing out or telling yourself this or that about what it all means, we just begin using the materials to assemble the greatest house that we could possibly build.

The discomfort comes from beginning to dismantle all of the walls that have built up throughout the years and identifying the internal lies you have been telling yourself. When you begin to see the dishonesty surrounding what you can and cannot do in life, it may be stressful . . . but beyond that stress, a world of possibilities will open up.

I clearly remember the day that I underwent a similar exercise surrounding the handcuff incident that I used as a reference in this chapter. There was an overwhelming sense that my entire life thus far had been a lie. That my life had been a waste up until now. This of course is an easy play for someone like myself that can see the negative much easier than the positive.

Be careful not to trade in one victim role for the next.

CHAPTER 2

Shifting from Victim to Victor

When you identify all of the situations that have occurred throughout your life that you may have been using to play the victim with others, and you clearly see how the reward you have been seeking pleasure from no longer—or never has—produced the payment you hoped for, you have built the foundation to achieve anything and everything.

What do I mean by this?

This chapter is devoted to explaining this, to leading you away from negative thoughts toward an unstoppable mindset. Having worked with thousands of clients, I know that the "victim" role-swap is not limited to just me. Based off my personal and professional experience, the most common mental play is for an individual to see the grave reality of one's situation and immediately start building a shelter to live within the walls of a victim role surrounding their new realization.

NO! DON'T DO IT!

Of course, I did what I am guiding you not to. So let me save you all the stress, procrastination, self-judgment, and all the rest of the negative thoughts that manifest from the realm of playing the victim again.

The next steps are to produce a shift in the way you view the role that you have been playing. Are you ready to break out of this deserted island of shattered dreams and procrastination? I know *I* was.

I am now going to guide you through a visualization exercise.

Visualization is nothing more than following a train of thoughts and incorporating as many senses as you can into the visualization. What does it feel like? What does it smell like? What emotions are you feeling within the visualization?

(I want to take this time to offer you an opportunity to go deeper. I've recorded a video series of the exercise that I am going to do with you. If you would like, go to **www.markcrandall.net/whyexercise** and I will guide you through this.)

Get into a comfortable position and close your eyes. Imagine that today is your last day on this Earth. Reflect on all the opportunities you gave up to the victim role you have been playing.

Don't get stuck on any one thing or go into morbid reflection on things that you have talked about doing but have yet to fulfill. Just notice specific areas or items and move on. Do not attach a story to them. Avoid *I should have . . . I could have . . . If only this had happened then . . .*

- Have you fulfilled tasks that you have been meaning to?
- Have you progressed professionally?
- Have you completed that one thing you have wanted to for years?
- What conversations do you wish you had?

Slowly come back, and when you're ready, open your eyes.

Now is your time!

You've certainly heard all the "here and now" slogans throughout the years. My favorite, and certainly the most common one, is that "there is no time like the present." So common, yet so true.

Do you want to know how I used the two exercises that I have outlined for you to shift my thoughts and become unstoppable?

Well, here we go.

Use Your Past to Create an Epic Life: The Only Three Things You Have Any Control Over

I have spent thousands of dollars on self-help books, courses, seminars, and coaching to hear over and over again that achieving your dreams is all about *taking action*. Well, that's great, but if you have self-doubt that creeps in every time you go to take action, then how much action are you really going to take?

If you're anything like me then you have or had a lot of half-started projects. When you live in a victim mindset, the most common thoughts that follow significant action are:

You can't do that.

Others can do that, but not me.

I'll just fail anyway.

What if they find out?

What will they think of me?

And on and on.

I have a running joke for this: I have a 100 percent success rate. I successfully start projects 100 percent of the time.

Are you tired of not completing the things you so badly want to do? Tired of carrying a to-do list around every day and feeling like it will never end?

For years, I have navigated my life from a *reactionary* mindset. A situation would arise, and I would react to it based on what in the moment I felt was the best response. The problem was not that I *reacted* to the situation; it had more to do with the mind state in which I was *seeing* the situation. I was constantly viewing tasks and situations from the mindset of *I can't because . . .*

Are you ready to start accomplishing your hopes and dreams?

I know I was.

Yes? Good!

Then let's create another shift in your mind.

We need to make your WHY much larger than your WHY NOT.

I've asked more people than I can count why they are doing whatever it is that they are doing in life. I would say that 90 percent of the individuals I have asked this question either have no answer or one that they are not truly satisfied with.

My WHY used to be: *I wanted to prove everyone wrong who said I couldn't.*

The truth to that, if I'm going to be honest, is that no one actually *said* that I couldn't—no one, that is, outside of myself. My own mind was the producer of more self-defeating thoughts than one man or woman could ever process. All of what I believed others thought was fabricated within my own mind. Sure, others told me that it would be hard to write my memoir, most people fail at building a company, and social workers don't make money. But none of those comments mean anything unless I myself *believe* them.

When I started to really evaluate my WHY, I began to feel overwhelming gratitude for all that I have gone through in life. I came to the realization that if I had been through all of the things I have in life already, and overcome them all, I could achieve anything.

I began to fuel my goals and aspirations with my past. My WHY, at first, was *I do not want to end up like my father*. This served me for a short period of time, but it wasn't accurate. My father is a great man. He did everything he could with the cards he was dealt and, I'm sure, inside of the scope of some victim role(s) he himself was trapped in.

My WHY needed to be bigger.

My limiting thoughts were still stopping me. My goals became bigger and bigger. Today my WHY is: *To show all of those still suffering from their past that anything in life is possible*. My WHY is to be a visual example that your circumstances in life do not need to determine your future. This WHY pushes me to get up at 5:00 a.m. when I don't want to, hit a stage when I'm terrified, post a video, go to a networking event, write my memoir *Eulogy of Childhood Memories*, write my self-help book *Embrace Your Past, Win Your Future*, and launch the Purpose Chasers Academy (which I share with you later in this book).

What is your WHY?

Most people, when asked what their WHY is, start spouting off a bucket list of tasks they want to complete or adventures they want to go on.

This is not a WHY!

These tasks may serve the mission of accomplishing your WHY, but they themselves are not it. For example, a few years back I wanted to write my memoir, speak onstage, and empower countless individuals to break free from their mental blocks to live the life of their dreams. But this does not have enough steam to get me out of bed early in the morning with enthusiasm.

Your WHY has to be *massive*. A tidal wave!

For a long time, I did not understand what people were talking about when they were describing their WHY. I can think of a well-known influencer whose WHY is to buy a major league sports team. I think this is great—but what happens when he *does* buy the team? His WHY shrivels up on the spot.

What is your WHY?

What mark do you want to leave on the world?

How will this impact others?

My suggestion would be that you pause the book and begin to journal about your WHY. You will need to have a basic understanding of what your WHY is before we enter chapter 3 of the book.

Procrastination

This section may prove to be the best collection of writing that I have done thus far. I'm stating this for myself, not necessarily for you, the reader. I've spent days and days of my life researching why humans procrastinate. After countless transformational workshops, self-help books, and hundreds and hundreds of coaching hours, I believe that I have solved the riddle.

If each day when you woke up and got out of bed, you imagined that this day could be your last here on Earth, would you choose to procrastinate?

NO!

Especially if you had broken free from your "playing the victim" mentality and established a strong WHY!

I have carried out the following exercise in individual coaching sessions, corporate group settings, and even from the stage of speaking events. The response is always strong, and my audience and/or clients seem to wake up to the reality that tomorrow is not promised.

(Again, I've granted you *FREE* access to a recording of this exercise at **www.markcrandall.net/whyexercise**.)

Think for a moment.

What is your number one justification for procrastinating?

"I'll do it tomorrow!"

"Tomorrow" is the only excuse that I've ever come up with for procrastinating anything in life. For years, I held myself back with thoughts of being the victim of the circumstances in my life. Yes, I had dreams of being an author and speaker; I had dreams of touching the lives of millions and leading the way for all of those who did not believe they could. But I found myself taking no action at all on my dreams. It was always *Someday I will . . .* or *I'm going to soon and it will surely be great*. It was as if I was waiting for all my hopes and dreams to just happen, without any action on my part. Deep down I believed that one day I would wake up and everything would have happened for me. That the world owed me this.

But it never did.

And because it never did, my self-esteem got smaller and smaller.

The goal of the following visualization exercise is to get you in touch with the *here and now*. To truly experience the power of each day.

This meditation does not need to be done perfectly—there is actually no such thing as a *perfect* meditation. This was merely designed to get your thoughts racing. Do not go down rabbit holes of the mind! The most common rabbit hole is one that involves negative self-talk.

Just visualize and see the thoughts as they are—like looking at the sky and watching clouds pass. You are where you are right now for a reason.

Get into a comfortable position.

Begin to walk through your day.

As you play it out, think about all of the highs and lows of your day.

Now imagine that someone approaches you. They state that they have extremely important news for you.

You inquire and they make you aware of the fact that at 5:00 p.m. tomorrow, your life will end. It's over. The curtain.

Begin to look over your life . . .

What do you wish you had done?

What do you wish you had said?

(Remember: avoid getting trapped in negative self-talk.)

Identify the areas where you wish you had taken more action.

What would you have said to that person if given another opportunity?

Have you fulfilled tasks that you have been meaning to fulfill?

Have you progressed professionally?

Are your relationships authentic?

Are there conversations you should have had in order to regain or maintain a connection that once was?

Don't get lost in any one thing or go into morbid reflection on things that you have talked about doing but have yet to fulfill. Just notice specific areas or items and move on.

Reflect for a few moments on the legacy you have left on this

Earth. Is this legacy made up of the person you have always wanted to be?

Now that you have seen the true extent of the fact that tomorrow is not promised, and procrastination is based off of the delusion that tomorrow *is* promised, how are you feeling?

A number of my clients have cried during this exercise. They have experienced all of the lost time in a way that they hadn't before. There is no such thing as lost time; rather, the time that you have not taken advantage of is your greatest asset as you continue on in this book.

In all of the transformational work I have done, I rarely take massive action when everything is going swell.

No, I take action when I identify that my purpose is much greater than I have been displaying in my life.

CHAPTER 3

From Scarcity to Abundance

Taking action used to sound and appear so painful. It was not until my WHY became so massive and my vision became so clear that taking action was no longer a chore. It became exciting.

My WHY began the process of using my past as fuel to create the future of my dreams.

The more work that I've done in the defining and refining of my WHY, the more opportunities opened up in my life. This sounds strange, I know, but it works.

Abundance Mindset vs. Scarcity Mindset

I've outlined in the previous chapters how I spent a majority of my life in self-doubt, operating out of a limiting belief system and in the process short-changing my hopes and dreams. Around the time that I broke free from my victim mentality, I was introduced to the idea of the Abundance Mindset. I had no clue what it meant at the time, but as in all areas of transformation, I quickly sought out to learn everything I could. Not only was I reading and listening to content, but I began to start to practice some of what I was learning as well.

I will start by defining the *opposite* of the Abundance Mindset: the Scarcity Mindset.

When a business mentor defined the Scarcity Mindset for me, I sat back in my seat. The definition caused me to swallow hard. He described the Scarcity Mindset as a state of mind in which we operate out of *fear*. Fear that there isn't enough work, money, or things in our life. We think, *My past will surely limit me from achieving this or that. My wife and I don't have enough money to buy a home or obtain our first investment property.*

I quickly realized that my entire life up until this point had been founded on the Scarcity Mindset. It drove my business decisions and shattered my dreams and aspirations in the process.

The Scarcity Mindset was running and ruining my life.

I asked my business mentor what this Abundance Mindset was all about, and he explained: the Abundance Mindset is all about changing your thoughts and words; these two things will change your actions, and therefore change what actually manifests in your life.

It sounded like some witchcraft, or a magic trick, not real. I was skeptical to say the least, but being the seeker of transformation that I am, I asked another question. I asked my mentor how I could shift my mindset from Scarcity to Abundance.

What happened next has revolutionized my entire life. He stated that I needed to use every situation, every event, every relationship from my past as fuel toward creating the future I really wanted.

I asked how to do that and was told to "start seeking!"

So I did.

I dove headfirst into studying the Abundance Mindset. My "A-ha!" moment came days into my studying. An Abundance Mindset provided me the direction to start walking down the hallway toward the light of my absolute potential. What I found was that I needed to start viewing my past as an *asset* instead of a *defect*. I needed to shift my mindset from "everything happens *to* me" to "everything happens *for* me."

This distinction rocked my world.

I began to see that everything from my past had built me into the strong man that I am today. Had none of these things happened, I would never have become a seeker of transformation; I would not have the work ethic I do today; I would not know how to read people as well as I do; I would not be so introspective; I would not serve as deeply as I do. I began to see how valuable my past actually was.

My past was my greatest asset!

Every morning, even now, I have reflected on and worked on changing the word structure surrounding my past. Instead of stating that things happened *to* me, I say "This happened *for* me." The longer I engaged in this practice, and the more my mindset changed, the more I saw others struggling with the Scarcity Mindset.

Do you want to break free from your own Scarcity Mindset?

Well, you can start right now. Take a situation from your past and state:

I'm so grateful that _____
because it _____
and has built me into the strong, driven, passionate person I am today.

I encourage you to write your own phrase so that this becomes personal and meaningful to you.

Example: I'm so grateful that <u>I was placed in state custody and later went to foster care</u> because it <u>taught me how to overcome any adversity and succeed no mater what the circumstances</u> and has built me into the strong, driven, passionate person I am today.

(Can you see that shift? "This happened *to* me" into "this happened *for* me!")

This is one of the most mentally challenging practices I have engaged in thus far on my transformational journey. The difficulty does not sit within the actual repeating of phrases; the difficulty lies in my mind's wanting to crawl back into the victim-cave it has lived in for years.

Just the subtle word swap of *this or that happened for me* versus *this or that happened to me* will trigger a mental response. Due to how long I have lived in the mindset of the victim, I find the resistance needs to be met with *persistence*. Meaning, once again, that this is a practice. A mental training camp, if you will.

Use this exercise to begin the practice of retraining your mind. The exercise you just completed needs to be written out on a piece of paper or sticky note and put on your bathroom mirror, another on your computer screen. Begin repeating this several times per day, multiple times each session. You will quickly see how these situations from your past have done more FOR you than they have TO you. If you want to overcome where you currently are, then you need to begin to counter how you have spent years thinking.

This is not a quick fix.

Pick at least four places where you will keep your new mantra.

Example of mine:

I'm so grateful that my childhood happened FOR me, because it has built me into the strong, driven, passionate person that I am today. I will use all of these experiences to fuel the actions I will take toward the future

I will have.

This is how you begin to turn your past into fuel to create the life of your dreams! ABUNDANCE!

Shift the way you view your past and your past will become your greatest resource in creating an EPIC LIFE!

If you take one thing away from this book, I beg you to take the action outlined above—even if your mind is telling you it is stupid and will not work. I *know* that it will, as it has worked for me and countless of my coaching clients.

You need to place reminders in all the places your Scarcity Mindset feeds itself throughout the day. Having sticky-note reminders will allow you to see and acknowledge the necessity of interrupting and replacing your old thoughts.

I have experienced a lack of food to eat, and I have experienced homelessness; I know what it is like to go without. And, believe it or not, I'm so grateful for all of these experiences. They have fueled my success in business and my passion for sharing my transformation with the world. I don't resist these thoughts when they arise; I embrace them, repeat my mantra, and use them as fuel to take action. I'm grateful for all the things that have happened *for* me, as they have built me into *who I am today* and *who I will become tomorrow.*

As with most books, workshops, seminars, therapy sessions, and any other attempts humans engage in to better their own lives, IT TAKES PRACTICE.

None of the breakthroughs that I am sharing with you here came out of the one-and-done method. You know what I am talking about: we read a book, and although there was information in it that makes us feel good, feel inspired, or we have a major realization, it all goes away quickly if not put into practical action.

As I have previously shared in my writing, I have committed to a life of transformation. This means that I have devoted my life to the practice of transformation. One thing that I have done consistently throughout my quest in transformation is *take action.*

The ability to walk through fear and limiting beliefs is a tool that has become massive for creating my life of purpose.

I have found that when the individuals I surround myself with play the victim themselves, or just plain live in constant negativity, this plays a massive role in whether or not I will be able to maintain my new mental shift. Because of this, I take who I spend time with and who I choose to surround myself with seriously. I cannot afford to go back to the mindset I crawled out of.

If I spend time with individuals who view themselves as victims, it will become much easier for me to fall back into that role myself.

I will go further into this issue in later chapters.

CHAPTER 4

Using Your Past as Fuel

For practically my entire life, I focused my mental energy on resisting things that I did not want. You know the thoughts:

*I **don't** want this job.*

*I **don't** want to go broke.*

*I **don't** want to pay my taxes.*

I allowed these thoughts to rule my life. They dictated almost all of my decisions. Whether consciously or unconsciously, these thoughts determined all of my actions day-to-day. Through introspection, it became very apparent that the more I resist the things I do *not* want to manifest in my life, the more these things *appear* in my life. This is due to the mental energy that goes into continuing the story of what the worst that could happen is.

A better explanation is this:

Thoughts = Feelings = Actions

Here is an even better example:

When my thoughts surrounding my past were negative, it created feelings of inadequacy, resentment, and low self-esteem; this caused me to take actions that were surely below my potential; I isolated myself, denied myself opportunities, and hindered my own transformational growth.

When I fear not having enough money, my mental energy is spent not wanting to pay bills, not wanting to buy things I need. All of my energy goes into how I can keep what I have versus channeling my energy toward abundance, which shifts my focus toward new ways of creating wealth in my life.

This shift may sound minor, but when you have spent ten to twenty years or more focused on scarcity, it is harder than it may appear. Not impossible—it just takes practice in training the brain and constantly disrupting thought patterns and replacing old beliefs with new, more abundant ones.

When my thoughts surrounding my past became positive, I began to experience an unstoppable flow of self-confidence; I began to see that I could do anything anyone else could achieve. People started to show up in my life, and amazing opportunities started to manifest.

Viewing Your Past as a Resource vs. a Liability

Unfortunately, when our thoughts are consumed with all of what we *don't* want, we usually end up getting exactly that. Even if the actual unwanted thing does not happen, we have already experienced all of the feelings surrounding it happening.

Really, though . . . isn't it all about feelings, anyway?

*I don't want this job because it makes me **feel** drained.*

*I don't want to go broke because it would make me **feel** unstable and insecure.*

*I don't want to pay my taxes because paying money in large sums makes me **feel** as if I am closer to going broke.*

It's all about **feelings**.

When it makes me *feel* good, it *is* good; conversely, when it makes me *feel* bad, it *is* bad. So why would I not start focusing my attention on the feel-good stuff? Why would *you* not?

With the Abundance Mindset, we shift our thought life (meaning the internal dialogue of our mind, you know the thoughts that dictate your actions or inactions) from living in the *unwanted* to the *wanted*. It is a practice. I've been at it for years now and still have thoughts linked to the above Scarcity Mindset.

Here is an example of my practice:

The fear is that I will go broke. So I repeat to myself the following:

"My wife and I have an abundance of wealth. We no longer fear paying bills or buying the things we want and need. This abundance creates joy within us both. This abundance of wealth eliminates our stress, diminishes our disagreements over spending, and, most importantly, allows us to serve the world on a much larger level. Our abundance of wealth allows us to buy our family nice gifts, donate to charities, and help out friends that may be struggling."

The above Abundance Mindset creates peace and security.

When I *live* in these feelings, I *attract* these things. New opportunities open up for me—new ways of generating income, new opportunities to serve. I am no longer forced to participate in things that do not produce these feelings. I can turn down jobs that I don't want. I can take a day off from work and just relax.

This practice has allowed me complete freedom from the fear I once lived in.

Here are some results over the last year of practicing the Abundance Mindset:

- Tripled my income (working for myself)
- Purchased my wife the home of her dreams

- Paid off all credit card debt
- Took multiple trips
- Paid all bills on time and without worry

To me, the practice of retraining my thoughts has been worth it.

This is how I trained my brain to use my past as fuel toward creating the future of my dreams. Who would have thought that the way I spoke to myself internally was the key to standing in the light?

I invite you to come stand in the light with me!

I know you have heard all of the catchy clichés, such as "What you think about is who you become" . . . but isn't this true? In my experience, it is. Again, when I am focused on what I *don't* want to happen, I attract or see all of the actions necessary to actually make that—what I don't want—become a reality.

It follows, therefore, that if I shift my mental energy in the opposite direction—what I *want* to happen—I get positive results.

You can do this too!

You will begin to see new opportunities, feel energized, and manifest the life of your dreams. This is not made up. It has been the teaching of all of the world's religions since the beginning of time.

Three Things We All Have Control Over

In life, there are only three things that we have any control over:

1. Action
2. Mindset
3. Reaction

Most people spend the majority of their time focused on things they have little to no control over.

For example, I have spent years and years focused on what others think about me. This is something I have no control over at all. The consequences of focusing on this have caused me a great deal of internal and external suffering. The thoughts manifest behaviors, and the behaviors manifest reactions.

Hopefully you are seeing the destructiveness of this endless circle.

Again, when I focus on what I don't want, those things end up entering my life. Whether that is an action, or just thoughts and feelings, it's there.

1. Action

Every day as an entrepreneur, I am faced with a decision when my alarm clock goes off.

- Do I get up, make some coffee, and attend to my morning practices?
- Or do I hit *snooze* and wait until the very last second to get up?

Action has been the cornerstone to my success. It became a cornerstone because I had experienced negative self-talk for so long that caused me to not take actions or to take actions that were not going to further my aspirations and desires.

I've always been a very strong starter. Meaning, I can take action to *start* a million different things, usually all at once. But I always lacked the follow-through of actually finishing a project that I started. My mind seemed to be a factory of excuses that I could give for why I hadn't finished most things I'd started; but the one that continues to creep up on me today is #2 of the keys to using your past as fuel to create the future of your dreams—that's my *mindset.*

Everyone has a mindset that dominates most all of the decisions that we make. As I've discussed already, thoughts lead to feelings and feelings dictate actions. When my mindset is that I can start anything but finish nothing, do you think I'm actually going to accomplish anything? NO! Of course not! What ends up happening is I start more things and still finish none none of them.

No one on Earth truly *lacks* motivation. It's true. Everyone on this Earth is a starter. People start things every day, myself included.

For example, writing this book. It's my second book, and I had been discussing its start for the past five months before actually writing it. I started it a week after initially discussing it the first time, then other things needed to be started. The end result was that I found myself with more things started and most, if not all, unfinished.

The starting and then stopping is attributed to my mindset. In my experience, there are always limiting beliefs that crop up that cause me to stop once I've started. These thoughts vary and are frequently changing, but are always tied into the compounding story that I've placed on circumstances in my past, which I outlined in the first couple of chapters of Part II.

The most common thoughts are tied to a belief that I am not adequate, or that no one will appreciate the content I am creating or the message I am sharing. Based off my experience, however, this is not true at all. I've had countless people share their appreciation for my first book (an earlier version of Part I of this book, *Eulogy of Childhood Memories*), and many have gone through my courses—some have even done group and individual coaching with me.

So why is it that I stop?

Well, because I have years and years of practice of starting things and then stopping. The start-and-stop process has diminished my self-esteem and also compounded more stories of my past.

In order to use our past as fuel to create the future of our dreams, we have to retrain our mind. I cannot emphasize this enough. It is not going to happen overnight.

I've been practicing the retraining of my mind since 2007—twelve years total at the writing of this book. I have attended countless workshops and hired the best coaches I could find in order to break through my limiting beliefs preventing me from living the life of my dreams. This world we live in is focused on the quick fix, but the truth is that this work is a practice, a journey. There is NO finish line.

2. Mindset

The reason why I did not start and/or couldn't finish things that I started was because I lacked the mindset to do so. The thing that most successful people do not tell you is that thoughts are the number one defeater of individuals. We experience them on a daily basis. It may be that we haven't identified these thoughts as a hindrance in our life yet.

When I first started my business, I landed a couple of transformational coaching clients, which relieved some of my financial fears (the basis of my third book). I decided that it was finally time to write my first book—my memoir. *Eulogy of Childhood Memories* is a title I had picked out years ago. Even my memoir was something I had started but never finished (until 2017).

I was working with a coach at the time, so in our session I told him that I was finally going to start working on this. It had been my dream for over ten years. I committed to a time that week that I was going to work on it. I had high hopes. My dream was finally going to become a reality.

The day I sat down to complete it, I became riddled with fear.

What will people think of me?

Will people even like or buy my memoir?

Will people think differently of me if they know my life story?

And blah, blah, blah it went, on and on.

Short version: these thoughts came on so strong that I did not start working on my memoir for a couple months. These thoughts took me right out of my WHY—my WHY of sharing my story with the world to help people heal and overcome any obstacles in their lives and become unstoppable.

Which brings me to number three of the only things you have any control of: reaction.

3. Reaction

My default reaction to these thoughts was to quit rather than utilize the tools that I had been taught and that I also teach others. So I did. I quit.

Quitting has always been easier for me than persevering and finishing what I set out to achieve. In many ways, quitting seems easier to all of us. The problem with "I'll quit" as an auto-response is that it intensifies the negativity toward myself within my mindset, which in turn limits my actions.

Let me break it down further.

EXAMPLE 1:

When your mindset is <u>strong</u> your reaction to obstacles is to continue

ACTION **MINDSET**  **REACTION**

EXAMPLE 2:

When your mindset is <u>full of limiting beliefs</u> your reaction to obstacles is to **STOP**

ACTION **MINDSET**  **REACTION**

As my transformational coaching business has grown, I have worked with countless clients with the same struggles. Most often, my coaching calls focus on the limiting beliefs that are stopping the individual from completing what they so badly want to do.

Do you have this experience? Wanting to complete something so badly yet continuing to get stopped over and over?

What's blocking you?

YOUR MINDSET!

Our mindset is the only thing that can and will block us. It stops us from taking action, and it stops the action once we do start taking it. I would go out on a limb and make the claim that everything that you have stopped doing is rooted in a belief system that you've adopted based off a situation in your past—better known as "playing the victim."

The victim role stops me over and over again. The only way I have found to smash through this is to continue to evaluate and replace these thoughts.

I'm going to share another limiting belief that plagued my progression in life for around five years. I'm sharing this so that you can place yourself in my shoes and identify your own limiting beliefs. Comparing your own experiences is not going to help you break free; identifying your own limiting beliefs while I'm sharing mine, however, *will* empower you to break free.

How the Scarcity Mindset Prevented Me for Years and Years from Breaking Free

I have spent thousands of dollars trying to "fix" myself over the years. Hundreds of self-help books, countless transformational seminars, and hours and hours on coaching calls and mastermind groups; I worked with at least a dozen therapists and obtained a master's degree and two clinical licenses.

All to discover that our minds are the only thing that can defeat us . . . and the most important resource we have.

On August 23, 2007, I was released from New Hampshire State Prison. I had spent two more years incarcerated than I should have, all for similar drug-fueled crimes as the ones that led to my previous sentences. This release was different from the last three, however. The difference was that the three previous times, I had high hopes for my "new life" after release. This time, though, I felt defeated, drained, and so far wrapped into playing the victim of my past circumstances that I couldn't see any light at the end of the tunnel. It was literally as if the end of the tunnel had been closed off.

I remember the thoughts that filled my mind as I was released from prison.

You are a convicted felon, dope addict, and drunk.

You can't hold a job.

You have no future.

You will probably end up homeless again, living in the woods with no one to talk to—or, if you're lucky, you will live paycheck to paycheck, struggling each day to make it in this life, because those are the cards that were handed to you.

Living in these beliefs about myself, I continued the daily practice of blaming others for the life I was living. It seemed much easier to blame others than to take action and begin breaking free.

It's kind of two-fold, though. I would say that the idea of engaging in transformational work to smash through these beliefs was not even on my radar. What I mean is, I knew of self-help gurus and such, but I didn't see my own value enough to make the investment to change. If you don't know what I mean here, I'm talking about investing financial resources in myself. Money!

Why? Because I was playing the victim and did not believe that I was capable of changing.

I clearly remember looking up seminars and courses that discussed so-called "breakthroughs." People were stating that they were able to shed the way they had been living and start living a life of purpose and passion.

Not me—I just couldn't see it. I was too badly damaged. The real belief behind this was that I truly did not feel like I was worthy of the investment.

My Scarcity Mindset was preventing me from investing in myself to *overcome* myself. I needed to shed the skin of playing the victim before anything else would be possible.

Investing in Ourselves is the Greatest Investment We Can Make

What's the point in spending money on bettering my life? Well, because most humans spend the money anyway. I know that *I* used to—whether it was new shoes, new clothes, the latest iPhone, the newest this or that. I was constantly seeking to obtain items that would make me feel good. All humans do this in some form or another.

Think about your own life. In what ways do you seek relief through spending?

My question for you is, why would you not invest money in the one thing that could change everything for you?

This question struck me hard back in 2008, when a coach asked me. Why was I so resistant to invest in my mind, body, and spirit?

I had just thought that life was going to improve and my life of transformation would just continue to progress. As if, once I made the declaration to devote my life to the transformational world, everything would just come to me. These were the thoughts that manifested from my Scarcity Mindset and from my view as a victim.

I'm not worthy of investing in myself, I thought.

The first investment that I made into my own mind, body, and spirit was *Awaken the Giant Within: How to Take Immediate Control of Your Mental, Emotional, Physical & Financial Destiny!* by Tony Robbins. I not only read the book but took the actions that were prescribed within the book. Not long after this purchase did I see the value of the $16 I had just spent.

My quality of life improved, my mindset shifted a little, I became more productive, and, most importantly, I was inspired. I began to see the value of investing in my mind. Unlink most who dabble in personal development, I didn't stop seeking. Most individuals read a book, or attend a workshop, and ride the high until they are back living the same as they were before their transformational experience. I don't stop. I keep seeking, keep investing in coaching, in workshops, in courses and books.

Why do I do this? Well, because it feels better and better the more I consume and the more action that I take!

Most people will never get to experience this shift in thinking. Most people may make a couple purchases but never truly see the value in the investment.

Making the Commitment

Hopefully you have followed the directions from the exercises I have laid out for you thus far. If you have, I'm certain that you have benefitted in some way from your investment. You purchased this book, took action, and saw results.

This is what happened to me years ago. Not long after reading my first self-help book, I realized that I wanted more and more of this. In that moment I devoted my entire life to transformation.

As the saying goes, there is no destination. The transformation and excitement of the ride is in the journey.

Some individuals have stated that I was crazy—insane for spending the money I have, the countless months of my life I've spent studying since making this commitment. When asked why, I always state "For the effect produced."

The effect produced from purchasing, studying, and practicing transformational work is the greatest feeling ever. The best part of it is, it doesn't wear off! Not like going out to buy a new pair of shoes. Yeah, sure, when you first buy them and wear them it feels amazing. But how do you feel after you scuff them? How do you feel after they get dirty? After you start to realize it's time to buy another pair? The buzz has worn off.

I have found that the more money I spend, the more time I study, and the more I practice, the greater the feelings and results that are produced in my own life.

Confronting Yourself Over and Over Again is the Journey

Throughout this book you have engaged in a number of exercises in which you have shifted your story surrounding various circumstances in your life. Whether it is something drastic like the example I shared, or a memory of being fired from a job, these can be used to fuel the building of the future you have only dreamed of.

When we rewrite the stories—from *happened **to** me* to *happened for me*—we begin to really tap into the benefits of our past.

If you have flip-flopped back and forth between the two of these, do not worry! You did not do it wrong. You have spent years and years of your life living from the mindset that this *happened **to** me*, and that mindset is not going to disappear overnight.

I myself have been practicing this since 2007 and still sometimes go right back into the victim story. But the more I practice shifting these thoughts, the more I train my mind to view these past experiences as assets versus defects, the easier it becomes, and the stronger the motivation.

Here is another example of a story I created surrounding some of my past actions, a story that was rewritten to fuel my future. Notice the points in my description where you would normally stop.

As was mentioned before in Part II, and in even more detail in Part I, my memoir, I spent several years of my life incarcerated for crimes committed to feed my drug and alcohol addiction. So, when I was released from prison back in 2007, I left with a title attached to my name:

Mark Crandall, convicted felon.

As soon as I was released from my sentence, I had an overwhelming feeling of a lack of hope for my future. In my mind, based off what I assumed society thought of the title behind my name, I believed that my future would be limited. Jobs that I would be able to get would not afford me the opportunity to succeed; housing that I would get wouldn't be that great. In my mind, my past was going to write my future for me. My past was going to build a box around my hopes and dreams and keep them trapped there for life.

The story surrounding my past was so ingrained in my mind that it was a daily battle for me. I don't believe a day went by that I did not have thoughts surrounding what others thought of my past. These thoughts led me to live a tiny life. The actions that I took to better my situation and my life were well below my potential.

I was a year out of incarceration when the transformation work that I had been doing had me engaged in some really deep introspection. I started dreaming again. I started asking myself "Why *not* me?" instead of "Why me?" Although it is a subtle difference, those phrases will cause actions that would lead into opposite directions.

The "Why not me?" became stronger and stronger. The more introspective transformational work I engaged in, the louder the cries to fulfill my dream of being a speaker and author. The problem was that these empowering thoughts were often silenced by my inner victim.

The "Why not me?" was quite often answered by the victim. It usually sounded something like this:

"Why not me?"

Well . . . because you are a convict, a drug addict who comes from a family of addiction. You have never achieved anything in life and are destined to merely survive this life.

The almost-daily battle of smashing out the limiting beliefs telling me that I couldn't do this or that became an engrained part of my mind. The more I practiced, the less I went down the rabbit holes that I had in the past. I began replacing the "You can't do this or that" with "Of course you can! Look at all you have already gone through!"

The first real action that went against the stance of my inner victim was applying for a job that I really wanted. I wanted to work for the State of New Hampshire at a youth detention center—a place in which I spent several years of my childhood. Of course, as soon as I had the thought to apply for this job, my thoughts started firing as they always did.

You will never get hired!

You're a felon!

They will know all about your past!

Why would you even apply?

I had taken a great deal of action to overcome my past, and even nearly finished my bachelor's degree in human services at this point. Yet, still, I was having these Scarcity Mindset thoughts

This example brings me to the next exercise. This exercise is similar to a pros-and-cons list. You put all of the pros of doing or not doing something on one side of a piece of paper and all of the cons on the opposite side. Well, this exercise goes a little deeper than that.

Ask yourself this question:

If I do not take any action and continue to allow these limiting beliefs to dictate my future, what will the results be?

Here is how I answered this question.

- I will stay trapped in a job I dislike.
- I will continue to tell myself I can't do things that I want to do.
- I will lose sleep thinking about my dreams of being a motivational speaker and author.
- I will spend the rest of my life trapped.
- My life will end and I will have nothing but regret.

Every time I answer this question when wanting to take action, the answer hits me hard. After I answer this question, I ask, "What is the worst that can happen?"

The answer is very commonly something like "They will say no," "I won't get the position," "They won't even respond," or perhaps, "They will find out who I actually am."

What's the truth, though?

"I definitely won't get the opportunity if I don't try!"

The exercise that I engage in is very simply a couple of questions.

- If I do not take any action and continue to allow these limiting beliefs to dictate my future, what will the results be? Simply put, what is the internal and external cost?

- What is the worst that could happen from taking action? And is that worse than the consequences of *not* taking action?

This exercise has never led me wrong. Staying in the limiting beliefs would cause me to stay in the same position in life, while taking action helps me actually find out what is going to happen versus continuing to invent a sob story about what would happen if I *did* take action.

See how silly this actually is?

I tell myself why I can't take action and then I tell myself what would happen if I *did* take action.

I mean, honestly, what is the worst that can happen from taking action? You get told no, which in itself is not even an end.

The only way for you to fail is to quit trying.

For years, I would build a story off of the answer I received. For example: *they said no, so that means that I will always be a convict and will not be able to ever stop doing the construction work.* When all that actually happened was that they stated they had already filled the position, so I needed to look elsewhere instead of just giving up.

Our human minds attach stories to everything.

Something that has been profound for me is the saying, "Three-quarters of my resentments are based off of conversations that I had in my mind."

Simply put: they never actually happened.

I hear something and attach all kinds of stories to the answer, which inevitably restricts my progress and limits my potential.

I attended a transformational workshop one weekend in search of a way to silence the inner victim forever. Well, it did that—and a whole lot more. What I received from this workshop was one of the greatest distinctions I have ever made. And here it is:

No one lacks motivation.

No one.

What they actually lack is the confidence in themselves to progress toward completing the things that they aspire to.

Let me simplify this for you.

What I'm stating is that no one lacks motivation, and that most people whom others would refer to as "unmotivated" are actually stuck in the past and playing the victim. Their self-judgment is what stops them once they start taking action.

Here is a joke I often make during my speaking gigs:

The joke is that I'm the greatest starter that I know. I can start ten things at one time. The problem lies with being productive and disciplined enough to actually finish the things that I start.

As previously stated, once I would start something and the tasks would become more and more difficult, my mind would start to tell me things from the victim story that I had been building on for years. You know the thoughts:

You're not good enough.

It's too hard.

It won't work out anyway.

It's a waste of time.

What I needed was traction. This next portion is about just that. Getting some traction and continuing to progress.

The thoughts that have limited you are going to be your greatest resource once you learn how to work *with* them instead of *against* them. There is good news and bad news as it relates to your limiting belief systems that are producing these thoughts.

The good news is that these thoughts and all of your past experiences in life, no matter how negative you've made them out to be, will become your greatest fuel toward creating the life of your dreams.

The bad news is that these thoughts will never fully go away. There will always be situations that trigger a thought response within your mind. So, you'd better learn to work with them if you want to build an epic life.

Another distinction that set me on a long path of introspection is: **Who I was or thought I was is no longer who I am.**

What I mean is that most people are limiting their futures because they are stuck believing that they are still who they thought they were in the past.

Here is an example:

When I saw that the job I was seeking in the youth detention center was hiring, my first thoughts were that I would never get it—not with my record. I had felony convictions that would never afford me an opportunity like that. In this state of mind, I was living in victim-mentality limiting beliefs. If I had stayed in these thoughts, I wouldn't have even taken the first action of filling out the job application and sending my résumé.

Most people can take those steps—and would—however, some would stay trapped in these limiting beliefs and think about doing it for a period of time until the thoughts of taking action went away. Worst case, though, is that the thoughts of taking action never go away and a person lives a life of regret.

This is actually my worst nightmare—that in my final days I will be lying there, regretting not taking actions during the time I had on this Earth.

I knew that my thoughts were not who I was, and that who I thought I used to be then was nowhere near who I was in that moment; this enabled me to not only fill out the application and send my résumé over—I don't know if that alone would have ever landed me the position—but I was so confident in who I had become that I also sent a followup email and made a phone call to the supervisor.

Working With Limiting Beliefs vs. Working Against Them

For a long period of my life, I worked against my beliefs.

Most of this time, I wasn't even aware of the fact that I was doing so. When thoughts that limited my true potential would crop up, I would graciously venture down the rabbit hole.

You know what I mean, right?

I'd really take on the role of playing a victim. Often times, this would involve self-judging thoughts—anything that would fuel the limiting belief and co-sign it so that it would appear to be a reality.

As I'm sure some of you are already aware, this is not conducive for accomplishing your goals and/or striving for your dreams. The initial limiting thoughts themselves are not bad at all. They are going to crop up. It is human nature to have thoughts, both negative and positive.

There is a process that I engage in to feed my thought life. When you have spent years and years feeding negative thoughts, you are going to need to take some actions and change some of your mental influences in order to create lasting change—and, more importantly, no longer go down the rabbit hole of self-judgment.

I'm a huge believer in the mind, body, spirit model of personal development. In it, we must feed all three areas equally to produce lasting change and continue to progress.

In short, I love the gym.

There was a gymnastic movement I had been working my butt off to conquer. It's called the "bar muscle-up." It is essentially when you pull yourself all the way over and on top of the bar. Countless members of my gym told me it was too hard, I was too new, it would come in time. I didn't listen to any of that noise. I watched video after video. I tried and tried. After about two weeks of practice, I got it.

Although everyone else in the gym told me it was hard, it would take time, blah, blah, blah, I decided to make the declaration in my mind, and through the words I spoke that *I was going to do it*.

I practiced until my hands bled.

I failed over and over again.

Then came the day a few weeks after starting my practice. It was after a workout with one of the classes of peers who had been crapping on my parade. I chalked up my hands and walked over to the pull-up bar. I looked at it with deep intensity and said, out loud:

"Today is the day that I will conquer you."

I jumped up and grabbed the bar. First attempt, I was over the bar, screaming with excitement. The coaches looked at me with as much shock as the rest of my peers.

What happened? I had been practicing what I've taught you throughout this book. I focused on what I wanted. I practiced. I constantly told myself it was possible, and BAM—it sure was.

Most humans have become trained to submit after failing. They try and do not succeed and call that a failure. The problem is that these failures pile up on us. They start to demolish our self-confidence. We begin to put a mask on of THE VICTIM. We hide behind these masks. We don't take risks, we end relationships, and we ultimately live meaningless lives based solely on failed attempts. No one has ever been successful in life trying a few times and then calling it quits.

Do you know how I have accomplished as much as I have in life? I've turned life into a game I play. I fail, and tell myself that didn't work, BUT, what did I learn? I then use the "what did I learn" to fine-tune my approach and try again with more experience.

If you practice this, YOU can accomplish anything too.

Repeat after me:

There is NO SUCH THING AS FAILURE.

"Failure" is a word reserved by those who have already quit. Outside of quitting—stopping, if you will—there is no failure. There is *trying* and there are lessons learned. *What did I learn?* and *How can I do it better?* Look over all your past experiences in your life. How much did you learn from all of the deepest, darkest moments of your past? I bet you have learned more than you've ever evaluated. Take a look.

I've learned valuable lessons from my drug addiction, childhood abuse, incarceration, and all of the darkest moments of my life. The main thing I've learned is that I'm unbreakable. I'm powerful beyond belief. I can do anything. Look where I came from and where I am now. There is no stopping me—or you.

WE can do anything by changing our perspectives and embracing our pasts. When we embrace our past, we can use it as fuel.

Fuel to WIN OUR FUTURE!

In the final section of this book, we absolutely need to lay out some systems to implement to ensure that the work that you put in stays in place.

CHAPTER 5

Circle of Influence

After I got my start in the realm of transformational work, I quickly realized that if I was going to transform my life I needed to really take a hard look at each and every day. During one of my coaching calls, I was asked who was in my "circle of influence." At the time, I didn't understand what this meant.

My circle of influence?

It was explained to me that a person's "circle of influence" is the five people that we spend the most time with. It did not take me long to fill the list with five individuals. I was then asked to evaluate each relationship in the following way.

1. How do they contribute to my life?

   This, of course, means: is this person adding value to my life? At the time, I had to honestly say that most of my list wasn't adding much value to my life. They were, in a sense, just there.

2. Are these individuals empowering or hindering my personal and professional development?

   Again, all but one of the individuals on my list were buzz-kills. They were constantly telling me that I can or can't do this or that. When I would have lofty ideas of what my next steps were going to be, they were always quick to state these thoughts/ideas were not possible for me—or that I wasn't grateful for what I had because I wanted more (which is a load of BS). Wanting a higher quality of life and the means to be able to contribute more to others has nothing at all to do with a lack of gratitude, unless it's from a place of greed. This was not the case for me.

3. Will the individuals in my circle of influence be assets or liabilities in me achieving my goals?

This question hit me hard. Never in my life up until this point did I believe that there was a possibility that some of the people I spend the most time with on a day-to-day basis could actually be liabilities.

After really analyzing each relationship, I was left with one individual who I believed was actually contributing to my life in such a way that I felt they were an asset. That means that four of the individuals I spent the most time with on a day-to-day basis were hindering the achievement of my goals.

This realization really caused me to swallow hard.

All week I contemplated what the next move was for me as far as these relationships were concerned. You can imagine what my mind was doing with the epiphany I just had.

The following week, when I got on my coaching call, my coach asked me to answer the questions for him. I had thought that he would surely judge me for my circle of negative influence, but that was not the case at all. Apparently, it's very common to have individuals surrounding you that are hindering your growth. He explained to me that most humans never even evaluate the quality of their relationships. They just go through life never really achieving what they hope for.

I asked what I needed to do next. (Remember, I had just spent an entire week formulating my breakups with all of the individuals I had identified in my life as hindrances to achieving my dreams.)

My coach then said something truly profound. He stated that I needed to replace these relationships with individuals who possessed the qualities that I felt would empower me to complete my goals. He explained to me that if I added these people to my life and worked toward nurturing and growing the relationship, that I myself would grow, and as a result of this growth I would naturally outgrow my old, hindering relationships.

And guess what?

He was correct!

That's exactly what happened to me. I went to networking events and seminars, and as I did I found new individuals with the qualities I needed in my life. I began to nurture these relationships, and as I did, my old relationships died off. That's not to say that I never spoke to the others again. That's not what happened at all. My old circle of influence saw that I was heading in a different direction and the relationships followed suit.

Have you ever heard the saying "Water seeks its own level"?

This is a basic law of attraction. You get what you give. Well, if I am negative and don't believe I can achieve much of anything, then I'm going to attract relationships that support this. When I'm positive and believe I am truly unstoppable, then that is what I will attract.

My circle of influence today is one of the most important aspects of my life. These individuals support, encourage, and challenge me on a daily basis. When I have negative beliefs that crop up, or bad days, I reach out to these individuals. They push me to move past it. When I say that I don't believe I can do this or that, they remind me that I can do anything.

This exercise changed my entire life.

The world I lived in shifted, and as a result I started to achieve my dreams.

My challenge to you is to do the same.

Evaluate your relationships. Start to fill your day-to-day life with the individuals you wish to emulate. When I started to surround myself with these types of individuals, I became the person I wanted to be.

A person who is truly unstoppable and views no goal as out of reach.

A person who believes his greatest asset is the darkest depths of his past.

If you surround yourself with those playing the victim, they will allow you to do the same.

But if you surround yourself with those achieving their dreams . . . think of the possibilities!

Once you've established a circle of influence and began to nurture these relationships, you naturally begin to implement one of the most under-utilized tools in our society.

Accountability!

"Accountability" is a word that is thrown around quite a bit in the realm of personal and business development. It is usually associated with goal-setting and objective-completion.

For those of you unfamiliar with the principles of accountability, when I set a goal, I then lay out a specific plan of action surrounding what it is going to take to complete the goal. I will share the goal and the objectives with my accountability partner(s), so that they know what objectives I am working on and by when I will have them completed. Just the sharing process alone will create a desire within to fulfill my objectives.

(Goal-setting and objective-completion are not things I will address in this book, as there is an abundance of information out there on how to set goals.)

Based on my experience coaching countless clients, I believe that an individual drops the ball on their hopes and dreams when it comes to accountability.

There is something that happens to me in my thought life that causes me to stop taking action well before the deadlines are completed. Limiting beliefs crop up, and if these limiting beliefs are left unchecked—meaning they are not identified, evaluated, and shared—then I can be stopped dead in my tracks.

The accountability that needs to be discussed is the sharing of the limiting beliefs, and how *just sharing* will get you back on track.

When I have limiting beliefs that crop up throughout my attempts at completing my goals, the first step is the identification of the limiting belief; from there, I can evaluate it.

The evaluation process is nothing more than the realization of the lie that I am telling myself and the actual truth. My mind tells me lies about multiple situations every day. These are hardly ever founded in any truth, but when these false beliefs crop up, if not evaluated and shared with someone else, they snowball into bigger thoughts and eventually turn into actions.

This happens because one thought turns into multiple thoughts, and as time goes on I start to actually believe these to be true.

Again, when you focus on the negative, the negative appears. You need to surround yourself with individuals who are thinking with an Abundance Mindset. If you surround yourself with these individuals, you will no longer go down the rabbit hole of negative thoughts.

Here is an example of the process that I have just outlined. I recommend that you use it as often as false beliefs crop up for you, as this will keep the thoughts at bay and you will stay in your flow state and accomplish anything and everything you desire.

A common limiting belief for me is that I can't do something because of my past.

When I evaluate this, I discover that my past plays no determining role in my present.

To gain accountability, I share this openly with one of my mindset accountability partners.

The outcome is thus: it's identified as dishonest thought patterns, shared with another human, and I continue on where I left off before these thoughts came into play.

This example brings me to the next chapter, and the main premise of this book: the distinction that how you speak to yourself is how you speak to the world. If you want to live an abundant life as the result of doing epic things, you must feed your thought life with empowering thoughts and surround yourself with empowering people. The individuals you surround yourself with are one of the main keys to you WINNING YOUR FUTURE!

CHAPTER 6

How You Speak to Yourself is How You Speak to the World

As I've stated over and over again in my writing, for years my growth and success was hindered by my lack of belief in myself. Outlined in the earlier chapters of this writing, I disclosed that most of my life had been living from distinctions I created in the past. While living my life from the past, I stayed stuck in the outcomes that were similar to what was received in the past.

It really felt like *Groundhog Day.*

For some reason, the realization that my internal dialogue dictated my external circumstances never clicked for me. Just what does this mean? Well, if I'm constantly telling myself that I can't do things, or this or that is out of reach, the chances of me achieving or even seeing the next set of directions toward achievement are slim.

Why? you may be asking.

Because I'm not *looking* for it.

When my thoughts are consumed with negativity, all I'm seeing is negativity. People are ONLY limited by their past when they believe they are still the same person as they were back then.

When you believe that you are a horrible person, you will show up in the world as a horrible person. You will attract other negative people and put yourself in negative circumstances.

Misery loves company.

I'm sure you've heard that before.

Let me ask you a question:

Do you want to increase your circle of influence?

Do you want to do a deep-dive into all of the exercises I've laid out in this book? Do you want to write massive goals and accomplish them? Do you want to learn how to love yourself, as I have learned to love myself?

Well, I wanted to create something that would allow all those who went through this collection of work the opportunity to go deeper. I have created a coaching academy to walk hand-in-hand with individuals who want to go much deeper than reading a book. Is this you? Do you want to go further? Really tap into and implement lasting change in your life?

Okay, okay, I hear you screaming *"YES!"* at me.

I have created the Purpose Chasers Academy (named after my Purpose Chasers Podcast on all podcast listening sites). It was created out of this collection of exercises and some more that I have not shared with you in this book.

If you want to go above and beyond where we have gone in this book, then I would encourage you to go to **www.markcrandall.net/pca** to apply to be enrolled in this epic six-week academy.

Don't apply if you are not ready to absolutely dominate your life and break through all of the limiting beliefs that are preventing you from being someone who WINS THEIR FUTURE!

In closing, I want to state that my writing of this book is to transform the way that our society views trauma and empower all those with traumatic pasts to learn how to change their stories and begin to embrace their past, just as I have. Don't allow anyone, especially yourself, to tell you that you cannot achieve greatness.

Anything, and I mean ANYTHING, is possible when you believe that it is.

Belief, followed by action, equals success.

Acknowledgments

The process of writing these accounts was one of the most difficult of my existence. To all of those who have been by my side since the beginning and those who stayed with me through the darkest times of my life, thank you; I owe you my life. Although many friendships did not make it through the trials and tribulations of my first twenty-two years, my family did!

It took some years to realize it, but I am truly blessed to have two sets of family. Both of whom supported me the best they could.

My rocks through this process are my most beautiful wife, Megan, and spiritual advisor, Brian. Megan, you have loved me through this process from the ups to the downs and back again. Brian, you talked me through some of the biggest fears I have ever experienced. You taught me how to be a man and demonstrated what it means to be a loving husband and father.

Marvin, I thank you for believing in me, loving me, and pushing me when I couldn't see the greatness within. Without you, this book would surely not have been written—nor would I be the man I am today.

Additional thanks to the men who have pushed me when I wanted to quit and who continue to take action in their own lives, helping to propel me forward; my mom and dad, Aura-Lee and Cliff, for taking me into your home and adopting me as your own and for being two of the most amazing souls I have encountered on this Earth; my sister Shannon, who has always been there for me and supported me no matter how I showed up to the relationship.

If I took the time to list everyone who has impacted my life, I would surely miss people, and I do not want to do that. If you have aided me in the process of becoming the powerful, God-reliant man I am today, thank you! I am truly blessed to know you.

In Part II of this book, I shared with you a series of exercises and perspective-shifts with the intention of producing transformation for each reader. I want you to know that I've been on an undying mission to shift my mindset since 2007. This is not an overnight matter. It will continue for my lifetime. One of the worst things that we teach in our society is that this is an easy process; that there is a quick fix, for which I searched for years and years and never found it. There is no "quick fix."

My journey has included countless workshops, weekend and week-long retreats, almost a dozen coaches, and a regimented spiritual practice. What I've found is that the more time, energy, and resources (aka money) that I invest in myself, the more empowered I become, and the greater my impact on the world becomes. You have made a great first investment by purchasing this book. I would encourage you to continue on this path for a lifetime. If you are interested in working further with Mark, then I would not hesitate to check out his Purpose Chasers Academy. This is a coaching program designed to go much deeper into the areas outlined in this book and empower the participants to start applying their learnings into their own lives.

Mark created the Purpose Chasers Academy *Because Your Dreams Should NEVER Be on Hold!*

If going further is something that you would like to take action on then feel free to visit Mark's other work:

Purpose Chasers Podcast:

www.markcrandall.net/purpose-chasers-podcast
Purpose Chasers 7-Day Jump Start: www.markcrandall.net/Jumpstart
Purpose Chasers Academy: www.markcrandall.net/PCA

About the Author

Mark's is a story of uncommon adversity and triumph. At age three, Mark was taken from his biological mother by the Department of Youth and Families and placed in the foster care system. He lacked the tools and supports to manage both his grief and his new reality in society's margins. From the pieces, he conjured stories about his own worth. At around age twelve, Mark began contemplating whether or not to just give up. Throughout his early childhood, Mark's behavior stood out to others as being abnormal and aberrant. He began to engage in criminal activity, acting out his aggression at the expense of those closest to him and society at large. Years of counseling and various combinations of medications could not correct the feelings of inadequacy and separation within. Mark began to self-medicate with substances; thus began his spiral into painful, chaotic addiction. Mark found himself in and out of youth detention centers and other correctional facilities. He lashed out at those who would protect and support him. Though, even in his lowest moments, Mark recognized what others saw:

There was greatness in even him.

In 2007, Mark found a spiritual program of action in which he began overcoming the many traumatic moments of his childhood. He also began the process of repairing the damage that he had caused others through his efforts to navigate life. Mark found freedom in an introspective process which informs his Transformational Life and Business Coaching and drug- and alcohol-interventions. Mark is trained in some of the most powerful transformation practices available, all of which he uses in his work with others.

With truth as a foundation, greatness grows tall.

Mark has re-written his story and has dedicated his life to empowering others to accomplish the same. Mark obtained a master's degree in social work (MSW) in 2014 and became a licensed chemical dependency counselor (LCDC) and licensed master social worker (LMSW). Mark spent seven years working with disadvantaged youth and providing individual and family counseling. He has conducted many successful Interventions for families in his work and has mastered the art of Transformational Life and Business Coaching. Mark is a master of conducting interventions and empowering the intervened client and the family to heal from drug addiction.

Mark's success as an entrepreneur has made him a highly sought-after Transformational Life and Business Coach. He and his carefully curated circle of Transformational Life and Business Coaches do not believe that anyone lacks motivation; what they may lack, instead, is vision. They recognize that with vision and the proper mindset, anything is attainable. Mark has proven this principle in his own life by building a six-figure company within five months of its start; by publishing his renowned first memoir *Eulogy of Childhood Memories*; by leading fruitful corporate workshops; and by inspiring a following through paid motivational speaking events.

Mark learned with the help of a long line of coaches that his past did not have to define his future. Mentors taught him how to break through real and imagined barriers and access greatness that lies within each living person. Mark considers his greatest assets to be his learned and organic abilities to bring out the potential within all of his clients and to guide them as they achieve their dreams.

Where to find more from Mark:

Purpose Chasers Podcast:
www.markcrandall.net/purpose-chasers-podcast
Purpose Chasers 7-Day Jump Start: www.markcrandall.net/Jumpstart
Purpose Chasers Academy: www.markcrandall.net/PCA